Pope Francis and the Joy of the Gospel
Rediscovering the Heart of a Disciple

POPE FRANCIS AND THE
JOY OF THE GOSPEL

Rediscovering the Heart of a Disciple

EDWARD SRI

Our Sunday Visitor Publishing Division
Our Sunday Visitor, Inc.
Huntington, Indiana 46750

For my daughter Chiara

Contents

Acknowledgments

I am grateful for the students, colleagues, catechists, and parish and diocesan leaders with whom I have been blessed to discuss various topics in Pope Francis' *The Joy of the Gospel* since its release in November of 2013. Particular thanks go to my colleagues at the Augustine Institute, especially Douglas Bushman, Sean Innerst, Lucas Pollice, and Jared Staudt for their feedback. I also thank Fr. Paul Murray, O.P., and Msgr. David Toups for encouraging me to pursue this project. And I am grateful for Alejandro Bermúdez with Catholic News Agency and Melissa Knaggs at *Lay Witness* magazine for inviting me to write articles on Pope Francis. Those articles served as the groundwork for this present book. I thank Cindy Cavnar at OSV whose editorial work helped make this a better book. Finally, I thank my wife Elizabeth for her prayers and encouragement throughout this process, especially during the editing that took place in the weeks surrounding the birth of another child.

Introduction

"This document is like an examination of conscience!"

That's how a number of friends — colleagues, priests, and laborers in the Church — felt upon reading Pope Francis' apostolic exhortation, *The Joy of the Gospel*. Many eagerly awaited this papal teaching, which was to follow up on the synod of bishops from throughout the world who gathered in Rome in 2012 to discuss the New Evangelization. Yet few of us anticipated how personally and spiritually challenging — and at the same time inspiring — the pope's exhortation would be.

Much of the initial media response, however, remained on the theoretical level. In both Catholic and secular media, many, for example, debated Pope Francis' statements about economic issues such as unfettered markets, wages, inequality, and "trickle-down theories." Others noted his strong critiques of abortion and consumerism. Still others focused on questions related to Church structure, such as the need for "sound decentralization," the role of women in the church, and the conversion of the papacy.

These and other important issues in the document certainly are worthy of further reflection and discussion. But we want to make sure we do not miss the more fundamental themes running throughout this exhortation and the ones the Holy Father himself states are his focus in this work (see EG 17). Pope Francis offers a message that challenges all Catholics — clergy, religious, pastoral workers, and ordinary lay people — *on a personal level* to walk ever closer with the Lord Jesus so that Christ's light might shine more powerfully through them. At its core, *The Joy of the Gospel* calls us to recover the heart of a disciple. It calls us to renew our daily encounter with Christ so that we can be disciples sent on mission — as "missionary disciples" — who share the joy of the Gospel in a world where many don't know the love of Christ.

A Retreat with Pope Francis

This book walks through *The Joy of the Gospel*, focusing on the themes that most directly relate to our call to live as missionary disciples — Christians who walk in *discipleship* with Jesus each day and who are on *mission* to share the love of Christ with the people God has placed in our lives. This is intended to be a highly readable book that draws out practical application of the pope's message in this exhortation. Think of *Pope Francis and the Joy of the Gospel: Rediscovering the Heart of a Disciple* somewhat as a retreat with the Holy Father for those who are inspired by his witness and teaching and want to live out his message more in their daily lives.

Along the way, we will see how Pope Francis' reflections, like those of a good retreat master, challenge us to constantly grow in our discipleship with the Lord, considering questions about our spiritual lives such as:

- Is my life truly grounded in a daily encounter with Christ — in prayer, humility, ongoing conversion, and an ever-greater surrender of my life to Christ?

- Do I see my identity in Jesus Christ, or do I seek fulfillment in success, financial security, comfort, human glory, or power?

- What might Christ be inviting me to give up that prevents me from following him more faithfully? My plans, my control, my pride, my fears, certain sins?

- Do I take time each day for "prolonged moments" of prayer, adoration, intimate conversation with the Lord, listening to His Word?

- Do I have hope, trusting in God's ability to work through difficult situations? Or do I often succumb to fear, worry, and discouragement?

- Am I patient with other people's faults, realizing how patient God is with my own?

- Do I eagerly extend Christ's mercy and compassion to others? Or do I tend to quickly judge people?

- Do I radiate the joy of Christ? Or do I tend to complain and focus on what's wrong in the world?

- Do I have an intense desire to share Christ's love with others? Or have I become lukewarm?

- How well do I fulfill my responsibility to care for the poor and most vulnerable?

- To what extent have I adopted a consumerist lifestyle that keeps me busy pursuing wealth, possessions, and amusements for myself while neglecting my duties to those in need?

- Do I truly encounter the people in my daily life — do I accompany family, coworkers, and friends amid their daily hopes and fears, joys, and sorrows? Or am I too caught up in my own life to notice others' needs and share in the trials and triumphs of their lives?

The Joy of the Gospel also encourages us to consider how well we live out our mission to the world — how much our parishes, our Christian communities, and our own apostolic works are animated by the Church's mission to share the Gospel . We can ask ourselves:

- Do we take the initiative to go out to people who don't know Christ's love? Or do we passively wait in our churches hoping they will come to us?

- Do we "take on the smell of the sheep," seeking to be involved in people's daily lives?

- Do we allow fear of change to keep us from doing what is best for the Church's mission?

- Do we avoid trying anything new out of fear of failure, fear of more work, or fear of having to humbly admit that what we have been doing in the past is not working?

- Do we feel trapped in "mere administration" and busywork that hinders us from sharing the Gospel with others?

- Are we disciples who surrender our lives to pursue the Church's mission? Or is our pastoral work shaped more by self-interest — what will bring us ease, comfort, control, or praise?

- Are we overly protective of our free time? Or are we generous in serving the Lord with our entire lives?

- Do we lovingly take time to prayerfully prepare our teaching? Or are we too busy?

- Are we disciples who radiate the joy and unity of Christian fellowship? Or do our Christian communities look like the rest of the world, fraught with envy, strife, battles for control, and petty arguments?

As we will see, *The Joy of the Gospel* is not a new theological statement about the New Evangelization, but a pastoral roadmap for how to implement it in our parishes, in our apostolic work, and most of all, in our daily lives. Francis himself explains that this document is not an "exhaustive treatise," but one that offers "practical implications" for the Church's mission today.

Let us now begin our journey with Pope Francis through this document, keeping in mind that his insights here should shape our lives. He emphasizes that this apostolic exhortation "is *paradigmatic for all the Church's activity*" (EG 15) and should "give shape to a definite style of evangelization which I ask you to adopt *in every activity which you undertake*" (EG 18).

Pope Francis doesn't just want us to study *The Joy of the Gospel.* He wants us to live it.

CHAPTER ONE

ENCOUNTERING CHRIST

The Call to Be Missionary Disciples

How would you respond to the very personal question, "Who are you?"

If someone asked me, "Who is Edward Sri?" I, like most people, would probably mention my work: I'm a theology professor, author, and speaker. I'd also tell of my family: I'm a husband and a father. And I'd highlight my faith: I'm a Christian, a Catholic, a son of God.

But I was surprised and deeply moved by the way Pope Francis described himself when asked in a 2013 interview, "Who is Jorge Mario Bergoglio?" He didn't focus on his work, his family, or even his Catholicism. He simply said, "I am a sinner. This is the most accurate definition. It is not a figure of speech, a literary genre. I am a sinner."[1]

To illustrate his point, Pope Francis referred to a famous painting by Caravaggio known as "The Calling of St. Matthew." It's on a wall in the Church of St. Louis of France in Rome, which the pope often visited. It's a beautiful scene that captures that pivotal moment in Matthew's life when Christ called him to become a disciple. Matthew was a tax collector — a shameful profession in first-century Judaism. Jewish tax collectors were known not only for taking too much money from the people, but they also were hated for being traitors, working for the Roman oppressors to collect money from their fellow Jews.

In the traditional interpretation of Caravaggio's painting, Jesus enters the tax collectors' lair and finds Matthew seated among his friends. Some are looking down, counting their money like misers, so caught up in their greed they don't even notice the faces of those around them at the table nor are they aware of Christ's dramatic entry into the room. Jesus brings light into the scene and points to Matthew, calling him to leave this dark world and follow him. Matthew points to himself, partly in disbelief ("You want such a sinner as *me* to follow you?") and partly in fear ("What is this going to mean for me? I don't know if I want to turn away from this life.").

> *"Here, this is me, a sinner on whom the Lord has turned his gaze."*
> — Pope Francis

Our "Money Bags"

The painting draws us into Matthew's profound encounter with Jesus Christ — an experience to which many can relate. We see Christ's merciful love seeking Matthew out in his darkness. We can imagine Matthew's mixed emotions: surprise, curiosity and wonder over the new path offered to him. And at the same time: the fear and shame over the part of him that clings to his sins and doesn't want to change. The painting brings us into that critical moment of decision for Matthew. What will he do? It's a snapshot of the turning point between Matthew the tax collector and Matthew the disciple.

Pope Francis said he is like Matthew at this moment of encounter. "That finger of Jesus, pointing at Matthew. That's me. I feel like him. Like Matthew." The interviewer described how, at this point, the pope became excited and determined "as if he had finally found the image he was looking for." Pope Francis went on to say:

It is the gesture of Matthew that strikes me: he holds on to his money as if to say, "No, not me! No, this money is mine." Here, this is me, a sinner on whom the Lord has turned his gaze. And this is what I said when they asked me if I would accept my election as pontiff.... "I am a sinner, but I trust in the infinite mercy and patience of our Lord Jesus Christ, and I accept in a spirit of penance."[2]

How moving is our pope's humble self-description! Our Holy Father instinctively identifies himself not with the saintly, post-conversion Matthew, the great apostle and Evangelist, but with Matthew the tax collector — the sinner who is afraid to let go of his sinful ways, the sinner upon whom the Lord turns his gaze, the sinner who entrusts his life to the mercy of Christ.

This Matthean encounter with Christ gets to the heart of the pope's apostolic exhortation *Evangelii Gaudium* — Latin for *Joy of the Gospel*. Pope Francis begins by challenging us to renew our personal encounter with Jesus Christ each day. "I invite all Christians, everywhere, at this very moment, to a renewed personal encounter with Jesus Christ, or at least an openness to letting him encounter them; I ask all of you to do this unfailingly each day" (EG 3).

Notice how at the start of this exhortation on the New Evangelization, Pope Francis focuses not on the many problems out in the world, but rather on challenging the faithful within the Church to renew their relationship with Jesus Christ. As we will see, it's as if the pope wants us to put ourselves in Matthew's shoes and encounter Jesus anew each day. The same Jesus who called Matthew to let go of his money bags continuously calls us to conversion and invites us each day to let go of whatever "money bags" keep us from fullness of life, whether it be our pride, our plans, our fears, our sins. And he waits with open arms to forgive us, heal us, and help us along the way.

It is in this daily encounter with Jesus — and only in this encounter — that we are liberated from the narrow confines of our self-centeredness and find true joy in life.

The Joy of the Gospel

But joy is something missing in many people's lives today. And that seems to be one reason Pope Francis titled his apostolic letter *The Joy of the Gospel*. He wants people to experience the joy of living for Christ and not for self — the joy of being freed from the sins that trap us in self-centeredness and discover the blessing of self-giving love.

What exactly is joy? According to St. Thomas Aquinas, natural joy is a fruit of love. It's the emotion experienced either in the presence of one we love or simply in the knowledge that the person is doing well. But spiritual joy is the fruit of the theological virtue of charity, love of God. It is experienced through our sharing in God's goodness. Therefore, to the extent that we live our lives participating in God's goodness — living for God and others in imitation of Christ — to that extent we experience deep, abiding spiritual joy. No matter what may be happening in our lives on the outside, we can still experience spiritual joy within through the love of God and living the way God made us to live, which is for self-giving love.

Modern culture, however, gets us to turn in on ourselves. Instead of living in service to God and others, we can become preoccupied with our own interests, comforts, careers, and pleasures. We feel compelled to constantly entertain ourselves, buy more stuff, and have more fun. But no matter how much we fill our lives with things, money, pleasure, or prestige, in the end we are left empty, restless, and searching for more. Pope Francis notes how this turning inward, this pursuit of wealth, things, and pleasure, leaves us more isolated from others and more closed off to God.

> The great danger in today's world, pervaded as it is by consumerism, is the desolation and anguish born of a complacent yet covetous heart, the feverish pursuit of frivolous pleasures, and a blunted conscience. Whenever our interior life becomes caught up in its own interests and concerns, there is no longer room for others, no place for the poor. God's voice is no longer heard; the

quiet joy of his love is no longer felt, and the desire to do good fades. (EG 2)

The Pope's Prayer

But this is a problem not just for non-Christians "out there" in the world. Pope Francis emphasizes that this self-centered life-style, so pervasive in modern culture, is a real danger for believers, too. He says, in fact, that "many" within the Church "fall prey to it." That's why he challenges the faithful to a renewed encounter with Christ, who alone can free us from our daily self-centeredness.

To help us encounter Christ anew, the pope invites us to recite the following prayer: "Lord, I have let myself be deceived; in a thousand ways I have shunned your love, yet here I am once more, to renew my covenant with you. I need you. Save me once again, Lord, take me once more into your redeeming embrace" (EG 3).

Two themes stand out in this prayer: humility and trust. Notice the humble honesty: "I have let myself be deceived;... I have shunned your love,... I need you.... Save me...." These words lead us to admit our weaknesses and sins and truly recognize how dependent we are on God.

But notice also the confidence in God's mercy: "Here I am once more, to renew my covenant with you.... Take me once more into your redeeming embrace." These are the words of someone who has experienced God's mercy and healing in the past and can entrust himself to the Lord again, confident in His saving help.

This daily, personal encounter with Christ's mercy liberates us from our self-centeredness and leads us to a happiness we could never experience on our own. "We become fully human when we become more than human, when we let God bring us beyond ourselves in order to attain the fullest truth of our being" (EG 8).

This also gets to the heart of why we evangelize: people who have experienced God's love and the profound liberation from sin as Matthew did are convinced that Christ makes all the difference in their lives. They know "it is not the same to live without him" (EG 121). Therefore, they have compassion on others and are driven to share what they have experienced. As Pope Francis explains, "If we have received the love which restores meaning to our lives, how can we fail to share that love with others?" (EG 8).

Missionary Disciples

Pope Francis insists that all the baptized have an important role to play in the New Evangelization. Sharing the joy of the Gospel is a mission for all the faithful, not merely for professionals with extensive training. While we might be tempted to categorize the faithful into two groups — *missionaries* who go out and share the faith and *disciples* who are passive recipients learning and growing in their faith — Francis says that all of us are called to be both: "missionary disciples" (EG 120). Any missionary who shares the love of Christ must first be a disciple, encountering him anew each day, experiencing his call to repentance, his merciful forgiveness, and his liberating grace. At the same time, anyone who has encountered the saving love of Christ in this way can begin to share that love with others. The first disciples, in fact, went forth right away to tell others about Jesus long before they completed their training with him (Jn 1:41) (EG 120).

Certainly, deeper intellectual, spiritual, and pastoral formation can help us offer a clearer witness to the Gospel. But this should not prevent us from sharing, in whatever limited ways and in spite of whatever human imperfections we possess, the profound reality we have come to know: the love of Jesus Christ. If someone happens to watch a great movie, he can go out and tell others about it. He doesn't need to become a professional film critic to share a good movie with a friend. Similarly, a married person doesn't need to go to graduate school before telling others why his or her spouse is so wonderful. We can speak from our experience of the love we have encountered.

And the same is true in our relationship with God. As Pope Francis explains, "In your heart you know that it is not the same to live without him; what you have come to realize, what has helped you to live and given you hope, is what you also need to communicate to others" (EG 121).

As we will see in the reflections throughout this book, much of *The Joy of the Gospel* is about recovering the heart of a disciple, or in the words of Pope Francis, rediscovering how to be "missionary disciples" — Christians who walk ever more closely in discipleship with their Lord and who thus have a profound sense of mission in this world. Indeed, discipleship and mission go together. When we become disciples of the Lord Jesus, evangelization is not some extra work or just one aspect of our lives. It flows from the core of our identity as followers of Jesus Christ. If we have encountered Christ's love — and continue to encounter him anew each day — we can't help but want to go out and share with others the joy we have experienced in Christ.

Questions for Reflection

1. Pope Francis is concerned that many aspects of the modern world lead us to turn in on ourselves. Caught up in our own interests and distracted by busyness, entertainment, and "frivolous pleasures," we fail to truly encounter the people around us and hear the voice of God. *What aspects of modern culture do you see encouraging us to close in on ourselves?* What are some specific ways you fall into this self-centered attitude? When you find yourself failing to give the best of yourself to the people around you, what steps can you take to resist that inclination?

2. Carravaggio's painting "The Call of St. Matthew" serves as a powerful image for Pope Francis' own Christian identity. Put yourself in this Biblical scene. Imagine Jesus suddenly coming into the midst of your daily life and calling you to follow him more generously. What might Jesus ask you to do or change or give up right now in your life to be a more

faithful disciple of his? What are you most afraid he might ask of you? What "money bags" (sins, attachments, areas of control) do you cling to?

3. Pope Francis has suggested we pray the following prayer daily:

> "Lord, I have let myself be deceived; in a thousand ways I have shunned your love, yet here I am once more, to renew my covenant with you. I need you. Save me once again, Lord, take me once more into your redeeming embrace." (EG 3)

What does it mean for you to renew your covenant with the Lord? To tell Him that you need him and to allow Him to embrace you? How might doing these things daily make a difference in the way you share the Gospel with others?

4. Consider making the above prayer by Pope Francis a permanent feature of your daily life. This week, pray it every morning, humbly coming before the Lord and admitting your sins and weaknesses and entrusting your life to Christ. Ask yourself now — and every day — in what ways you are shunning his love?

CHAPTER TWO

WHAT IS THE NEW EVANGELIZATION?

New Paths for a New Situation

The first time Pope St. John Paul II used the term "new evangelization" was during a dramatic visit to Poland in 1979.[3]

Picture the scene. It's his first time as pope to return to his native country of Poland, still under the atheistic regime of the communists. He goes to the modern suburb of Krakow called Nowa Huta, which represented the ideal communist city — a city without God. Nowa Huta is Polish for "new steelworks," and the city was designed to be the perfect industrial metropolis, featuring steel factories five times larger than the historic center of Krakow and massive apartment blocks for 40,000 people.

For the communists, Nowa Huta pointed to a new Poland, one that they hoped would erase the memory of the country's rich Catholic history. It was a sociological experiment — constructing an entire modern town that celebrated work and promised a better life, but a life without religion. It was the first town in the history of Poland built intentionally without a church, and the authorities did all they could to keep it that way.

But ever since he was made an auxiliary bishop in Krakow, Karol Wojtyla had fought against this atheistic ideology, and he chose Nowa Huta as a focal point in the struggle for Poland's soul. Every year, starting in 1959, he celebrated a Christmas midnight Mass for the workers in an open field there. He told the people that one day a church would be built in this town despite the authorities' restrictions on religious freedom.

In 1960, he defended workers who erected a cross as a reminder of their missing church. When the authorities threatened to tear it down, thousands of people took to the streets in protest. The government asked the young auxiliary bishop to tell his people to stop rioting. Wojtlya complied with their request and asked the people to maintain peace. But, much to the chagrin of the communist leaders, he also told the people there would be no reason for protest in the future because the cross would not be removed again! And then he told the government leaders that the only way to ensure peace in Nowa Huta would be for a church to be built for its people.[4]

After years of Wojtyla's persistence, the government eventually yielded, granting permission for a church, and Wojtyla consecrated it in 1977. By that time, he had become the Cardinal Archbishop of Krakow, and the church's consecration represented a victorious moment in the struggle for faith in communist Poland. At the church's dedication, Cardinal Wojtyla noted how the presence of a Catholic church in the supposedly religion-less town of Nowa Huta was a clear sign that the Polish people's true Christian identity was not forgotten. "This city is not a city of people who belong to no one.... This is a city of the Children of God [and] this temple was needed so that this could be expressed, [so] that it could be emphasized...."[5]

Two years later, Karol Wojtyla returned to Communist Poland for the first time as pope. During his historic nine-day visit, he went back to the Nowa Huta area and celebrated Mass at a Cistercian abbey on the outskirts of the town. It was in the homily for this Mass that he used the expression "new evangelization" for the first time.

The pope first recalled how this particular abbey housed a relic of the true cross of Christ that has been a point of Christian pilgrimage for many centuries. Such a treasure was made possible by the evangelization of Poland long ago when crosses were erected throughout the land as a sign that the Gospel had been welcomed by the people with love. Pope St. John Paul II noted that the cross, therefore, was a sign of the first evangelization of the Polish people.

> Where the cross is raised, there is the sign that evangelization has begun. Once our fathers raised the cross in various places in the land of Poland as a sign that the Gospel had arrived there, that there had been a beginning of the evangelization that was to continue without break until today.[6]

But then he recalled how the almost two-decade struggle to build a church in Nowa Huta also involved a cross — the cross that the steel workers there "raised as a sign of their will to build a new church." In the face of the communists' atheistic ideology that was attempting to remove religion from Polish life, the modern cross of Nowa Huta stands as a sign of a new period of evangelization for the Polish people. "In these new times, these new conditions of life, the Gospel is again being proclaimed. *A new evangelization* has begun, as if it were a new proclamation, even if in reality it is the same as ever. The cross stands high over the revolving world."[7]

Pope St. John Paul II's first use of the expression "new evangelization" was focused on the evangelization of Poland in particular. But it can shed much light on what John Paul meant when he later called for a new evangelization for the rest of the world. Like the Church in Poland facing the forces of atheistic communism, much of the Church around the world faces new ideologies and ways of life that undermine faith — even in countries that were previously marked by the cross of Christ. In some cases, it might involve government authorities destroying churches, arresting priests, outlawing religion, or, as was the case in Nowa Huta, Poland, tearing down crosses.

But in other settings, a culture of consumerism and incessant entertainment dull the spiritual life and stifle the pursuit of virtuous living, while the pervading influence of secularism keeps people from thinking much about God in their daily lives and the "anything goes" mentality of moral relativism leaves people without an ethical compass for their lives.

Poland and other communist countries weren't the only places in the last century where crosses and traditional Christian values were being threatened. That happened in the secular West, too. Perhaps the only difference is that the Polish people of Nowa Huta fought to keep their Christian identity more than many of us do in the West. The people in Poland at least knew the communist regime was a threat to their well-being. But many today don't see the rise of secularism, relativism, and materialism as something that harms the human family. Many welcome it.

That's why modern secular countries in the West need a "new evangelization" just as much as Poland did under the communists.

Though there has been a lot of talk about the New Evangelization, many Catholics are unsure what it really means.

These cultures may be filled with people who have heard of Jesus and the Catholic Church, people who might be baptized, and even people who attend Mass, but as Pope St. John Paul II notes, they live their lives "far removed from Christ and his Gospel."[8] They are shaped more by the secular world around them than they are by the Gospel. A new evangelization is needed to face this new situation.

Hence, it is fitting that Pope St. John Paul II later took this idea of a "new evangelization" that he first articulated in Poland and applied it to the Church's mission in the rest of the modern world. Throughout his pontificate, he called on the Church to bring a new evangelization to the many cultures in the modern world, "where entire groups of the baptized have lost a living sense of the faith, or even no longer consider themselves members of the Church" (RM 33). The splendor of the Gospel message must be re-proposed in new ways that attract those who have rejected or brushed aside the faith. And he made this a most urgent priority for the Church, saying, "The moment has come to commit all of the Church's energies to a new evangelization" (RM 3).

Pope Francis' *The Joy of the Gospel* can be seen as one of the many fruits of Pope St. John Paul II's call. In October of 2012, bishops from throughout the world gathered in Rome for an extraordinary synod to focus on the theme of "The New Evangelization for the Transmission of the Christian Faith." *The Joy of the Gospel* is Pope Francis' apostolic exhortation that draws together key insights from that gathering and outlines the approach to the New Evangelization that he wants the Church to pursue.

But what, exactly, *is* the New Evangelization? Now that we have some background, let's take a closer look.

Exploring the New Evangelization

Though there has been a lot of talk about the New Evangelization, many Catholics, even among those working within the Church, are unsure what it really means.

When I ask an audience at a Catholic conference or parish event, "How many of you have heard about 'the New Evangelization'?" I'm impressed by how many people raise their hands — many more than a decade or two ago. Yet, when I proceed to ask the audience, "Who can explain what it is?" practically all the hands go down. The few people who attempt a response typically say something like, "It's about sharing the faith with great fervor," or, "It's about using technology and the media to teach the faith." Or even, "The Church is finally starting to evangelize!" So, while there is increased awareness of the term, few seem to possess a clear understanding of what it actually means.

The Two Areas of Traditional Evangelization

Evangelization is nothing new to Catholicism. The Church has been evangelizing ever since its conception almost 2,000 years ago. The Church has one mission, which is to evangelize — to bring people into communion with Jesus Christ, "the source of

authentic personal fulfillment" (EG 10). So what is so *new* about
the New Evangelization?

Traditionally, the Church has carried out its evangelizing
mission in two main areas. First, there is the mission "*ad gentes*,"
a Latin expression meaning "to the nations." The focus here is on
the non-baptized. This is what most Catholics in the past probably had in mind when they heard about evangelization or missionary work. Typically this would involve a missionary going
overseas to China or Africa, for example, to proclaim the Gospel to a non-Christian culture — to people who did not know
about Jesus Christ or the Catholic Church. There, the missionary would give an initial proclamation of the Gospel, which was
meant to inspire in the people an interior conversion of heart
and lead them into the communion of Christ's Church through
baptism and the other sacraments.

Second, the Church also carried out its evangelizing mission by deepening the faith life of those who already committed
themselves to Christ. This was known as the mission of "pastoral
care." The Church has described this particular group of people
as being "fervent in their faith and in Christian living" (RM 33).
They have "said 'Yes' to Jesus and trustingly abandoned their
lives to Him."[9] They also have a "profound Christian outlook,"
meaning they view the world from the standpoint of faith with
Christ's standards in mind (GDC 58), and they "bear witness to
the Gospel" and have a "commitment to the universal mission"
of the Church (RM 33).

For these people who already have been evangelized and
are in need of pastoral care, the Church aims "to inflame the
hearts of the faithful" (EG 15) — to deepen their adherence to
Christ through prayer, the sacraments, and life in the Christian
community and to "make evangelizers of those who have been
evangelized" (GDC 58).

The New Situation

In which situation does the Catholic Church primarily find itself
in the United States? Would most parishes in our country be

considered places where the mission *ad gentes* needs to be carried out? No. Most people who come to Mass are baptized and have at least heard about Jesus Christ and the Catholic faith.

But would we portray the state of the Catholic Church in this country merely as a situation of pastoral care in which we simply need to deepen the faith life of those who already have firmly committed themselves to Christ and the Church? When I ask parish and diocesan leaders around the country if they would describe the average parish as a place where the people are "fervent in faith and Christian living," where they have surrendered themselves to Christ, and where they have a profound Christian outlook — almost all the leaders say, "No."

So the Church in the United States (and much of the modern world) finds itself in a new circumstance. There are large groups of people who may be baptized, who may call themselves Catholic, who may go to Mass every once in a while, or who may go every Sunday. They might even serve on a parish committee, sing in the choir, teach children's catechesis, or be a Eucharistic minister. But they have not yet had that initial conversion of heart and surrendered their lives to Christ. And they do not have a "profound Christian outlook."

While there are plenty of opportunities for mission to the non-baptized (mission *ad gentes*) and still many fervent Catholics who want to deepen their communion with Christ (mission of "pastoral care"), the Church now faces a new situation that does not fit either of these two general categories. There are many people who may have some real connection to the Catholic Church, but their lives are influenced more by the secular, individualistic, and consumerist culture than by the Gospel. They tend to evaluate critical moral issues more according to what they watch on television and the relativistic attitudes of the people around them, for example, than by the teachings of the *Catechism of the Catholic Church*. Their understanding of what success is, what makes us happy, what love is, what true beauty is, what a good marriage is, and what the meaning of human sexuality is comes more from Hollywood and the popular media than from what Jesus Christ and the Church teach about these things.

Indeed, as Pope St. John Paul II explained, some Catholics, even though they may be practicing their faith to a degree, have "accepted a secular model of thinking and living" and thus "live a life far removed from Christ and his Gospel" (RM 33). And this is not a small, insignificant segment of the Catholic population. "Entire groups of the baptized have lost a living sense of the faith," John Paul said (RM 33).

In her book *Forming Intentional Disciples*, Sherry Weddell notes that the majority of baptized Catholics in the United States, for example, have drifted away from practicing the faith. Of those raised Catholic, 38 percent call themselves Catholic, but seldom attend Mass, and 32 percent no longer identify themselves as Catholic at all. These are all people who have Catholic roots, but who, in the words of Pope Francis "do not reflect the demands of Baptism," and "who lack a meaningful relationship to the Church and no longer experience the consolation born of faith" (EG 15). Similarly, according to a study conducted by the Center for Applied Research in the Apostolate (CARA), 77 percent of Catholics identify themselves as proud to be Catholic, but only 23 percent regularly attend Mass each week. This indicates a clear disconnect between faith and life for many who call themselves Catholic.[10]

> *It's not "business as usual" in the Church.*

The New Evangelization is the Church's response to this situation in which large numbers of baptized Catholics, some of whom may even be active in their parishes, have not had an initial conversion, surrendered their lives to Christ, and allowed the Gospel to shape their lives. These are the baptized who have not encountered Christ in the life-shaping manner that Matthew the tax collector did. The New Evangelization is new not in the sense of offering people a new Gospel message, but new in terms of the intended missionary outreach that includes not just those who never heard the Gospel before (mission *ad gentes*), but also the lukewarm and non-practicing in cultures that previously were Christian but have now become secularized. In the words of Pope Benedict XVI, the New Evangelization consists of re-proposing the Gospel to people in regions "where the roots of Christianity are deep but who have experienced a serious crisis of faith due to secularization."[11]

New Ardor, Methods, and Expression

The New Evangelization is also new in terms of the "ardor, methods, and expression"[12] that are needed for the Church to respond effectively to this situation. Pope Francis challenges us to consider new pastoral goals that make evangelization the top priority of all we do in the Church and new approaches that are capable of reaching the many whose lives are not shaped by the Gospel.

As the preparatory document for the 2012 synod of bishops expressed, it's not "business as usual" in the Church. We cannot cling to the way things have been done in the past if those programs and approaches are not drawing more people into communion with Christ.

> A New Evangelization is synonymous with mission, requiring the capacity to set out anew, go beyond boundaries, and broaden horizons. The New Evangelization is the opposite of self-sufficiency, a withdrawal into oneself, a *status quo* mentality, and an idea that pastoral programs are simply to proceed as they did in the past. Today, a "business as usual" attitude can no longer be the case. Some local Churches, already engaged in renewal, reconfirm the fact that now is the time for the Church to call upon every Christian community to evaluate their pastoral practice on the basis of the missionary character of their program and activities.[13]

Synthesizing insights from this Synod, *The Joy of the Gospel* is not a new theological statement, but a fresh pastoral roadmap for how we are to implement the New Evangelization in our families, workplaces, communities, parishes, dioceses, and apostolic work. Though not "an exhaustive treatise," the document has great importance for how we are to live out this mission in our daily lives.

Let's now walk with Pope Francis through *The Joy of the Gospel* and discover how we can give our lives more fully to the New Evangelization as missionary disciples. And may we have the courage to consider new approaches that are capable of reaching the many who do not know the joy of friendship with Christ.

Questions for Reflection

1. First, let's review: What are the two traditional areas in which the Church carried out its evangelizing mission? When did the Church first begin to speak about the need to rethink the traditional categories of evangelization?

2. What is the new situation the Church faces today among the baptized? Why does this new situation not fit the two traditional categories for evangelization?

3. How would you explain what's *new* about the New Evangelization? Prepare an "elevator speech" that describes the New Evangelization and at the same time captures the joy of the Gospel.

4. How do you think the New Evangelization influences the way we should teach the faith? Does it make a difference in the way you present the faith to those you meet, or to your family, or to those you teach if you are in pastoral ministry?

CHAPTER THREE

A CHURCH WHOSE DOORS ARE OPEN

Going Out to the Peripheries

Pope Francis says he wants a Church "whose doors are open" (EG 46).

When I first heard this statement, I assumed he was calling for the Church to be more welcoming — a warm, friendly, compassionate environment that receives everyone, no matter what their background and no matter what perspectives, lifestyles, and weaknesses they may bring. Others might have pictured volunteers cheerfully greeting people as they come in for Mass, signs outside the Church inviting people to the parish, or hospitality committees making new parishioners feel at home.

These may be aspects of a welcoming community, but Pope Francis is thinking of much more.

When he describes the "open doors" of the Church in *The Joy of the Gospel*, he is not thinking only about how we let people in. The open door is not about one-way traffic — outsiders entering our churches. Pope Francis wants the doors open so that we within the Church will dare to *go out* — to step out of our offices and the walls of our comfort zones to go out to the world to bring the saving love of Jesus Christ to those on the edges of society.

"Go Out" or "Come to Me"?

Pope Francis envisions a Church that goes forth. He notes that all throughout salvation history, God calls his people to step outside of themselves, to move beyond what is secure and familiar in service to His plan. God called Abraham to go to a new land. He called Moses to lead the people out of Egypt. He asked Jeremiah to call people with hard hearts to repentance.

Jesus himself went forth from Nazareth to proclaim the Gospel, filled with an urgent desire to share the love of God. "Let us go on to the next towns, that I may preach there also; for that is why I came out" (Mark 1:38). Pope Francis describes how Jesus was continually pressing forward, going outward, to spread the good seed of the Gospel. He sows the seed, but then He moves on, prompted by the Spirit (EG 21).

> *Jesus didn't pass out flyers inviting people to a Bible study on the beatitudes.... He made it a priority to get involved in people's lives.*

And Jesus called his disciples to do the same: "Go therefore and make disciples of all nations, baptizing them in the name of the Father and of the Son and of the Holy Spirit, teaching them to observe all that I have commanded you" (Matt. 28:19–20). This missionary mandate continues as Jesus calls all his followers today to participate in the Church's evangelizing mission and go and "make disciples." The particular path and expression of evangelization may look different from Christian to Christian, but "all of us are asked to obey [Christ's] call to go forth from our own comfort zone in order to reach the 'peripheries' in need of the light of the Gospel" (EG 20).

Let's consider that key word "go." Jesus showed his disciples that evangelization should not be about waiting for people to come to us, but about going out: "Go therefore and make disciples of all nations."

A temptation for many ministries in the Church, however, is to focus efforts on a "Come to me" approach instead of a "Go out" approach. Many groups simply schedule events, meetings, retreats, and conferences and then wonder why more people don't come. Outreach involves little more than making announcements at Mass, handing out flyers and advertising through the parish bulletin, email, and Facebook. "Come to our meeting!" "Join our group!" is the usual message. And very few new people show up; just the regulars who come to everything else the parish offers.

> *"The shepherd had ninety-nine sheep in his flock and went out to search for the one that was lost; we have one in the flock and ninety-nine that we are not searching for."* — Pope Francis

Organizing events, making announcements, and using social media can be tools in our evangelizing efforts, but they're not at the heart. Jesus didn't pass out flyers inviting people to a Bible study on the beatitudes. He didn't announce that he'd be in Galilee giving a talk on prayer and suggest people sign up. He didn't organize healing services and have his disciples issue invitations. Instead, Jesus went out to seek the lost. He made it a priority to get involved in people's lives.

The Art of Accompaniment

This "going out" might involve talking about our faith with complete strangers, whether it be the person sitting next to us on the plane or another parent at the park. And if we're involved in an outreach ministry, we will certainly find ourselves with opportunities to speak of our faith with strangers. Pope Francis, when he was a parish pastor in Argentina, encouraged his brother Jesuits in formation to go out and look for children to invite to catechism classes, to knock on doors and to visit families in the neighborhoods.[14] As archbishop of Buenos Aires, he had a large tent set up in the main plaza next to the city's train station where priests could talk to the people passing by. Many stopped to ask questions, seek a blessing, get spiritual direction, and even go to confession.[15] Archbishop Bergoglio even suggested that priests should rent garages in those zones of the city between parishes and send a layperson there "to spend time with people, give religious instruction, and even give Communion to the sick or to those who are willing."[16]

For many years before becoming pope, Francis was emphasizing the need to go out and meet people, to live out the parable of the Lost Sheep. Underscoring the fact that many Christian communities neglect this responsibility, he said: "The shepherd had ninety-nine sheep in his flock and went out to search for the one that was lost; we have one in the flock and ninety-nine that we are not searching for."[17]

But in our fast-paced world that emphasizes activity, this call to "go out" should not be interpreted as an overeager desire to build new outreach programs, start new groups, or make an impersonal proclamation of the faith to "the world." Pope Francis, rather, is calling us to invest our lives in other people, removing our sandals "before the sacred ground of the other" (EG 169). This is something anyone who has encountered Christ can do. It involves compassionate listening, getting to know others, serving them, and sharing with them the joy and consolation that comes from friendship with Jesus Christ.

Going out of ourselves to personally share Christ's love with others can also happen quite naturally with the people God has placed in our lives — in our families, schools, workplaces, and communities. Pope Francis calls it an "informal preaching" that can come easily in conversation (EG 127).

When we sincerely enter into other people's lives, listening to their hopes and dreams, their fears and sorrows, we discover opportunities to show how God's Word can shed light on their situation and offer them encouragement and hope. We may also find moments when we can humbly share from our own experience the ways that the Gospel has made a difference in our lives. But these windows in evangelization usually open wider only after we have truly accompanied people in their daily lives and they have sensed our compassionate heart (EG 128, 169–171). "Often it is better simply to slow down, to put aside our eagerness in order to see and listen to others, to stop rushing from one thing to another, and to remain with someone who has faltered along the way" (EG 46).

I wish I had understood this important point during my career with a company in the corporate world.

I had only worked with this company for about two years when I decided to leave the job and begin graduate studies in theology as a layman. I liked the company, enjoyed my work, and was blessed to have several good friends there, but I found myself spending all day thinking about the Catholic books I was going to read when I got home at night or what I was going to do at the parish that evening with the youth ministry group I was helping lead or the adult faith formation classes I volunteered to teach. I really liked my job, but there was a deeper love pulling at my heart. I knew I needed to go.

I told my boss, and he sent out an email to all the members of my department informing them that I was leaving the company to "study Catholic theology." It just so happened that all 120 of my colleagues would be at headquarters that week for a corporate retreat. So as we traveled together to beautiful northern Michigan for various team-building exercises and strategy meetings, the news of my departure was a frequent topic of discussion: "Did you hear Ted is leaving next month? And he's leaving to go study Catholic theology! Is he becoming a priest?"

But the timing of the announcement coinciding with the corporate retreat also sparked many conversations. I found myself spending a lot more leisure time with my colleagues, getting to know them on a more personal level, learning about their families, their hopes, their struggles, and their fears. I also found myself constantly having conversations about faith. People opened up to me about very personal things — struggles in their marriages, regrets about the way they raised their children, battles with cancer, questions about Catholicism, doubts about God, feelings of guilt over leaving the church, sins from their past. As the week went on, I felt somewhat like a priest hearing people's confessions!

There was a common thread in many of these conversations. Whether Catholic, Protestant, or not affiliated with any religion, these men and women — who were very successful and appeared to be happy and to have it all together — were searching for something more in their lives. All were on a journey of faith, and though I had been with most of them at the corporate headquarters day in and day out, I hadn't even noticed.

After dozens of these conversations, it became clear to me that all of these men and women wanted to grow in their relationship with God and to better understand Him and Christianity and life. All were longing for someone with whom they could talk about their lives. So on the last night of this corporate retreat, I invited them to come together to pray. When people trickled into the meeting room after dinner, each person looked around, surprised to see who was there. It was a simple prayer meeting. People opened up and shared their needs with the group, and then we would pray for that person's intentions. Nothing fancy or emotional. It was just a group of coworkers sharing what was going on in their lives and praying for each other's needs. But in that hour, the corporate retreat started to feel more like a Christian retreat. And people were grateful to know there were others who could walk with them on their journey of faith.

This is one of my most blessed memories of my time with the company. But I also remember experiencing some regret that day. I had been very involved in my parish helping with the youth group, confirmation classes, and adult faith formation classes — all comfortable settings in which people were seeking formation and coming to parish events. Yet the Lord had placed people in my daily work environment who were searching, people who were longing for someone to take an interest in their lives and listen to them, people who were hungering for Christ's love. They just needed someone to take the initiative, get involved in their lives, and start the conversation of faith. I was too busy to notice, however — too caught up in my own work at the parish to see the people right around me.

While grateful for what the Lord did in those days, I also wish I had lived out what Pope Francis describes — the need to go out. This going out doesn't have to mean preaching on the streets or traveling to a distant land. It can simply mean going out of ourselves and taking the initiative to be more involved in the lives of the people God places in our midst, truly accompanying them in life, and then, when appropriate, in the natural flow of conversation, sharing how the joy of the Gospel can shed light on their life situation.

This is something simple every disciple of Christ can do. It opens doors for sharing how friendship with Jesus Christ makes all the difference for our lives, leading us to happiness and eternal salvation. It also is something parishes and faith communities can easily encourage and train their people to do.

Questions for Reflection

1. *Evaluate your community:* Consider your parish as a whole or your particular small Christian community (whether it be a men's or women's group, a Bible study, your family, or another small faith community): On a scale of 1–10, with 10 being the highest, how well does your community reach out to those on the peripheries of Catholic life — those whose lives are not shaped by a personal encounter with Jesus Christ?

2. *Identify the obstacles:* What do you think prevents your particular community from being closer to 10? What fears, inadequacies, or dysfunctions keep your community from serving the Church's evangelizing mission more?

3. *Plan for Improvement:* What can your community do practically to move closer to 10?

CHAPTER FOUR

CHARACTERISTICS OF AN EVANGELIZING COMMUNITY

The Church's Missionary Conversion

Is your faith community — your parish, your small faith group, your apostolate — truly a community that goes forth? Or is it a community that is more focused on itself and the same twenty, fifty, or two hundred people who already come to everything? How do we know if our faith communities are living out Christ's missionary mandate well? Pope Francis offers several characteristics of an evangelizing community for us to consider.

1. Taking the initiative to seek those who have fallen away.

The model here is God himself. God did not stay up in heaven, waiting for us to fix our sin problems. He loved us first. He came down from heaven, entered into our world, and became one of us. And throughout his public ministry, Jesus didn't focus his outreach on the ones already well connected in Jewish society — the priests, the Pharisees, and the Sadducees. Rather, Jesus sought the lost, the sinners, the poor, the suffering — all the outcasts in first-century Judaism.

Take, for example, two stunning chapters in the Gospel of Matthew, Matthew 8 and 9, which showcase Jesus' urgent desire to bring light to all the dark corners of Israel. First, he reaches out and touches a leper — a man who was considered ritually unclean and had been expelled from society. In so doing, Jesus heals him not just physically, but also restores him to the social life of the Jewish community.

In the next scene, Jesus converses with a Roman centurion, an officer who commanded a large number of soldiers and who would have been viewed as a great enemy of the Jewish people. Not only was he a gentile — a non-Jew — who was considered unclean, he was also a *Roman* centurion, a leader of the very army that was oppressing the Jewish people. Yet Jesus dialogues with this man, heals his servant, and praises him as having more faith than anyone in Israel.

Jesus continues on the move, healing Peter's mother-in-law and then casting demons out of many. Driven by his concern for the lost, he crosses the Sea of Galilee and enters the predominantly gentile territory of the Gadarenes, where he expels demons from two men. He comes back to Galilee, where he moves from town-to town, eats with tax collectors and sinners, heals the blind and the lame, raises a girl from the dead, heals a man with a withered hand, and expels more demons.

Notice that Jesus didn't sit inside a synagogue hoping people would come to him, he stepped out with energy and purpose. Pope Francis reminds us that we are to do the same. "An evangelizing community knows that the Lord has taken the initiative; he has loved us first (cf. *1 Jn 4:19*), and therefore we can move forward, boldly take the initiative, go out to others, seek those who have fallen away, stand at the crossroads, and welcome the outcast" (EG 24).

This kind of going out is not easy, even for people in pastoral ministry. People who work in parishes have told me, "It's easy to share the faith when someone comes to my office or to my program. I'm comfortable with that. I know how to evangelize when they come into my world. But if I have to go out into their world, I don't know what to do. We've never been taught how to evangelize."

2. An endless desire to show mercy.

Throughout his public ministry, Jesus was intent on showing mercy. He forgave the sins of the woman who, in tears, kissed his feet (Luke 7). He forgave the paralyzed man brought to him on the stretcher and the woman caught in adultery. He mingled with tax collectors, prostitutes, and other sinners who were rejected by Jewish society. He even forgave his enemies from the cross, saying "Father, forgive them; for they know not what they do" (Luke 23:34).

An evangelizing community doesn't show mercy to others out of duty, because this is what good Christians are supposed to do, but because we have personally *experienced* God's mercy ourselves. As Pope Francis says, "Such a community has an endless desire to show mercy, the fruit of its own experience of the power of the Father's infinite mercy" (EG 24). It all comes back to our personal encounter with Christ. If we regularly encounter Christ as Matthew the tax collector did — if we are truly aware of our own sins and weaknesses and experience Christ's forgiveness and the power of his grace liberating us from our selfishness — then we will want to share this new life, this joy of the Gospel, with others. As St. Catherine of Siena once explained, "The love a soul sees God has for her, she in turn extends to all creatures. She immediately feels compelled to love her neighbor for she sees how fully she herself is loved by God."[18]

If, however, we don't truly come to terms with our own sins and weaknesses, we will tend to look down on other people's faults. We might pride ourselves on following the truth: on being more orthodox and more morally upright than the rest of the world. We might pat ourselves on the back because we practice a certain devotion or voted for the "right" political candidate. But if we fail to face the truth about *ourselves* — if we fail to encounter Jesus daily, humbly acknowledging before him that, in the words of Pope Francis, "I have let myself be deceived; in a thousand ways I have shunned your love" — then we will tend to be very impatient with others who may struggle with faith and may not share our moral convictions. Instead of responding with an eager desire to share the Gospel and show them the compassion and mercy of Christ, we set ourselves on a comfortable moral high ground unwilling to imitate Jesus, who met people where they were.

Instead of evangelizing, we make evaluations from afar: "They don't believe X." "They didn't go to Mass last week." "They have the wrong moral views."

3. Getting involved in people's daily lives.

Evangelizers are not detached from the people they serve — they invest their lives in those people. A community of evangelizers, therefore, "bridges distances, it is willing to abase itself if necessary, and it embraces human life, touching the suffering flesh of Christ in others" (EG 24).

> "The Holy Father told me at the beginning: 'You can sell your desk. You don't need it.'"

In one of the most celebrated lines from *The Joy of the Gospel*, Pope Francis says true evangelizers are so immersed in people's daily lives that they "take on the 'smell of the sheep'" (EG 24). They accompany people in the midst of their daily lives (EG 169). They know people's hopes and dreams, their fears and sufferings, their questions and their doubts. As such, the sheep are willing to listen to their voice.

From the perspective of the sheep, the voice of the evangelizer is not that of an outsider instructing, imposing, critiquing, making judgments, and giving unwanted advice. Such voices from afar are usually politely brushed aside, ignored, or opposed. Rather, the shepherd has so personally invested himself in the sheep that the sheep, hearing his loving voice and knowing he cares for them, respond.

Pope Francis, when he was archbishop of Buenos Aires, was known for going out and spending time with the poor and homeless, taking them food and sitting on the streets with them to share a meal and talk. Now, as Pope, he is encouraging his staff in the Vatican to do the same.

Take, for example, what Francis told Fr. Konrad Krajewski, the Vatican "Almoner" — the one in charge of handing out alms to the poor around the world. "The Holy Father told me at the beginning: 'You can sell your desk. You don't need it. You need to get out of the Vatican. Don't wait for people to come ringing. You need to go out and look for the poor,'" Krajewski said. "This is the concept: Be with people and share their lives, even for fifteen, thirty minutes, an hour."

> *Evangelizers should take on the smell of the sheep more than the smell of their office furniture.*

He went on to describe how the Holy Father "would go out at night in Buenos Aires, not just to find people, talk with them, or buy them something to eat.... He would eat with them. He would sit with them and eat with them on the street. This is what he wants from me."[19]

Pope Francis' giving of himself to the poor in this way, sharing life with them, is a model for evangelization — for sharing the joy of the Gospel with the *spiritually* poor. His words to Father Krajewski and his own personal example challenge us to examine, on one hand, how much time we spend in the familiar confines of our offices, committees, and email, and on the other hand, how much time we spend with the people themselves.

But reaching out to others is not always part of the average parish staff culture, according to some who work in the Church. Attending meetings and organizing successful events may be praised, while outreach may not be as appreciated or may even be subtly frowned upon as not productive. As one parish worker told me, "I feel judged sometimes for talking with parishioners, spending time with them during the day, trying to get to know them better. I get looks or questions: 'Where were you? Why were you not in your cubical or in meetings?'" Pope Francis, however, challenges us to make a paradigm shift. Evangelizers should take on the smell of the sheep more than the smell of their office furniture.

4. Patient, apostolic endurance.

Are we looking for immediate results? Are we discouraged or frustrated when people don't seem to be progressing in faith as much as we'd like? Pope Francis reminds us that evangelization requires what he calls "apostolic endurance." It consists mostly of generous patience and does not fit timetables. When people take a few steps forward and a few steps back, true evangelizers thank God for the good in people's lives and don't focus on the stumbles. "The sower, when he sees weeds sprouting among the grain, does not grumble or overreact. He or she finds a way to let the word take flesh in a particular situation and bear fruits of new life, however imperfect or incomplete these may appear" (EG 24).

Evangelizing communities understand human weakness and encourage people, even in their struggles, to live the faith. Rather than become impatient with slow progress, faults and failures, they're always supportive, "standing by people at every step of the way, no matter how difficult or lengthy this may prove to be" (24).

5. Filled with joy.

No one wants to hear the Good News from evangelizers who look like they've just come back from a funeral (EG 10). True evangelizers radiate the joy of Christ.

Far from being pessimists, focused on the problems in the world and lacking confidence in God to bring good out of difficult situations, they place their hope in the Lord and trust in His timetable, not their own. With patient, apostolic endurance, an evangelizing community always rejoices in what God is doing, grateful for even the smallest signs of growth. Such a community "celebrates at every small victory, every step forward in the work of evangelization" (EG 24).

Missionary Conversion

The word conversion means to turn around, to turn back. It is often used to describe non-believers becoming Catholic or people in sin turning back to the Christian path. Pope Francis, however, uses this word to challenge the whole Church to "convert" — to go in a new direction in terms of how it views evangelization.

Evangelization is often thought of as just one of the many things the Church does. However, it should be the other way around. Everything the Church does should serve the mission of evangelization. The pope, therefore, calls for "a pastoral and missionary conversion" that permeates the entirety of the Church's life and has "programmatic significance" for all the Church's activities (EG 25).

> I dream of a "missionary option," that is, a missionary impulse capable of transforming everything so that the Church's customs, ways of doing things, times and schedules, language and structures can be suitably channeled for the evangelization of today's world rather than for her self-preservation. (EG 27)

Pope Francis challenges us to examine our faith communities. Are our structures and activities truly dedicated to evangelizing the world or are they primarily at the service of "self-preservation"? Do we tend to look inward at serving our own interests and the kind of people with whom we like to socialize? Do we close in on ourselves, falling into "a kind of ecclesial introversion" (EG 27)? Or do we have a constant desire to go forth?

Pope Francis notes that parishes have a particular role to play in the New Evangelization. Parishes are meant to be "the Church living in the midst of the homes of her sons and daughters," he tells us in paragraph twenty-eight of *The Joy of the Gospel*, but he challenges us to ask how well the parish is fulfilling this role. Is the parish "really ... in contact with the homes and the lives of its people," or is it "out of touch

with people"? Is the parish truly "a community of communities, a sanctuary where the thirsty come to drink in the midst
of their journey, and a center of constant missionary outreach?" Or is it more of a "self-absorbed group made up of a
chosen few"?

When a parish fails to go out, when it fails to encourage and
train its members to be evangelizers, the community of believers
loses vibrancy and closes in on itself, serving only a small circle
of people who might be more interested in what they get out of
the parish for themselves (whether it be fellowship, affirmation,
interesting conversations, or the comfort of being around like-
minded people) than they are in evangelizing the world around
them. In this sense, such a community reflects Matthew the tax
collector's inward turn — looking out for its own interests —
more than Christ's urgent desire to search out the lost and enter
into their world with his love.

Focusing parishes on evangelization will take time. Some
progress has been made since the Second Vatican Council, but
Pope Francis makes it clear that many parishes have a long way to
go. Too many, he says, are not in close touch with the people and
are not centers of vibrant relationships and active involvement in
parish life (EG 28).

Sell Your Desk?

Does this mean we should all sell our desks and evangelize full-
time on the streets? Not at all. Those in administrative roles that
serve the ongoing formation of the faithful, for example, may
need to do much of their work inside the office walls of the parish. Still, Pope Francis says "mere administration is not enough."
He challenges all pastoral workers to do more than administrate.

First, anyone in a leadership role, whether it be as a Bible study
leader, a parish catechist, a pastor, or a diocesan director, should be
forming the people they serve in a way that inspires and equips them
to evangelize. If the regulars who come to our parish events are not
themselves going out to share the faith and draw others into the par-

ish life, that's a sign that something may be lacking in the way we are forming our people. We want to build an evangelizing community, not a self-enclosed community.

Second, Pope Francis' vision for the Church challenges all pastoral workers to find some area outside their comfort zones where they can step out to give themselves personally to those on the peripheries. If Pope Francis, even when he was a busy archbishop, could take time to share his life with the poor on the street, then pastoral workers can also find time to give not just a program, but themselves, personally, to people hungering for the joy of the Gospel. And if we are going to effectively train others to evangelize, we must be evangelizing at least to some extent ourselves. We cannot give what we don't have.

Which Fear Motivates You More?

In one of his most pointed challenges to those working in ministry, Pope Francis invites us to ask what motivates us more: protecting our own security — our own interests, comfort, and careers — or the fear of not sharing Christ in a world starving for his love?

> *Personal comfort. Fear of more work. Fear of failure.... Are these good reasons not to try new approaches to evangelization?*

In other words, will we try new ways to truly go out to the world or will we allow our fear of the extra work or fear of making mistakes entrap us in the security of our offices and committees?

Will we be willing to re-think how we pass on the faith? Or will we cling to what is safe and familiar because "that's how we've always done it"?

First, Pope Francis lays out the vision: "I prefer a Church which is bruised, hurting and dirty because it has been out on the streets, rather than a Church which is unhealthy from being confined and from clinging to its own security" (EG 49). Then he issues the stinging challenge:

I do not want a Church concerned with being at the center and then ends by being caught up in a web of obsessions and procedures. If something should rightly disturb us and trouble our consciences, it is the fact that so many of our brothers and sisters are living without the strength, light and consolation born of friendship with Jesus Christ, without a community of faith to support them, without meaning and a goal in life. More than by fear of going astray, my hope is that we will be moved by the fear of remaining shut up within structures which give us a false sense of security, within rules which make us harsh judges, within habits which make us feel safe, while at our door people are starving and Jesus does not tire of saying to us: "Give them something to eat" (*Mk* 6:37). (EG 49)

It is *not* business as usual. The pope says we can't leave things as they presently are. Mere administration of the Church as it is today is not enough. He exhorts us to reject the complacent mentality that fears new approaches. We must ask ourselves: Why do we keep using the same programs and approaches year after year, even if the way we've been doing things is not attracting new people to the Gospel?

There may be various factors at work. For many people, change is scary. Mediocre is safer than different. Others fear that new methods or new initiatives mean more work. "It takes a lot of time and energy to try something new," some pastoral workers have told me. "Our plates are already full. How can we add on something new?" Others fear failure. If something hasn't been tried before in the parish, there's risk that it won't succeed. Some pastoral workers don't want to let down their boss, their pastor, or their bishop. It's safer to stick to the normal models and not risk taking the blame if a new idea doesn't succeed. Finally, some people resist trying new approaches because they don't want to admit that what they have been doing in the past is not working.

But let's think about these motives. Personal comfort. Fear of more work. Fear of failure. Fear of having to admit a gap in my own abilities and leadership. Are these good reasons not to try new approaches to evangelization? These motives are not driven by mission, but by self-interest. Pope Francis, as we will see in greater detail in chapter eight, challenges us to examine our conscience regarding what really drives our decisions about what we do and how we spend our time in our apostolic work.

But here, he simply challenges all of us to think "out of the box": "I invite everyone to be bold and creative in this task of rethinking the goals, structures, styles and methods of evangelization" (EG 33).

Questions for Reflection

Pope Francis says he wants a Church that does not passively wait for people to come to us. He wants us to step out of our "comfort zones" and "go out" to those who do not know the saving love of Christ. Let's consider practically how we can live out this summons:

1. First, what does a Christian community that "goes out" look like? In other words, what are some of the key characteristics of an evangelizing community?

2. Second, what do you think hinders people from evangelizing more? What are the fears and inadequacies that typically keep people from sharing the faith with others?

3. Now let's take this on a personal level: Vatican II teaches that the laity should be "on the lookout" for opportunities to share the Gospel in the ordinary circumstances of their lives (see CCC 905). Consider the people God has placed in your life — in your family, workplace, parish, neighborhood, and so forth. Who around you does not know the joy of friendship with Jesus Christ? Take time to pray for those people and to ask the Lord for opportunities to share naturally how the Gospel can shed light on their lives.

CHAPTER FIVE

THE HEART OF THE GOSPEL

Our Message in the New Evangelization

Pope Francis created quite a stir in interviews he gave in the fall of 2013, sparking much conversation among Catholics and non-Catholics alike about the future of the Church and his papacy. His comments, for example, about abortion, homosexuality, and contraception were celebrated by some and feared by others as a radical departure from Catholic moral teaching.

The pope's comments, no doubt, have been controversial. But the key to interpreting Francis' statements properly is found in his vision for the Church. As we have seen, the Holy Father wants a Church that doesn't just open its doors to others, but goes out to the world: to those Christians who are indifferent, to the Catholics who stop going to Mass, and to unbelievers. This outward, missionary-styled focus shapes the way the Gospel message is presented to the world.

> *"When helping the seriously wounded on the battlefield, it doesn't make sense to focus on people's cholesterol and blood sugar levels."*
> — *Pope Francis*

In his interview with Fr. Antonio Spadaro that appeared in *America* magazine, the pope described the Church as a field hospital for the suffering. When helping the seriously wounded on the battlefield, he says, it doesn't make sense to focus on people's cholesterol and blood sugar levels. First, we heal their most serious wounds. "Then we can talk about everything else," he said.

Similarly, many people today do not know the Gospel of Jesus Christ, and as a result they suffer serious wounds. They do not know that Jesus loves them, has saved them, has a plan for their lives, and wants to bestow His mercy upon them and offer a life much better than what they experience without Him. This is the initial proclamation that people need to hear. The heart of the Gospel is the *saving love of Jesus*, not "gay marriage and abortion are morally wrong" or "contraception separates the unitive and procreative aspects of marriage." It is in this sense that Pope Francis said in the interview, "We cannot insist only on issues related to abortion, gay marriage and contraceptive methods" and that "it is not necessary to talk about these issues all the time."

Some Catholics responded to this statement by Pope Francis with confusion or frustration, but Pope Benedict XVI articulated the same idea in 2006:

> I remember, when I used go to Germany in the 1980s and '90s, that I was asked to give interviews and I always knew the questions in advance. They concerned the ordination of women, contraception, abortion and other such constantly recurring problems.
>
> If we let ourselves be drawn into these discussions, the Church is then identified with certain commandments or prohibitions; we give the impression that we are moralists with a few somewhat antiquated convictions, and not even a hint of the true greatness of the faith appears. I therefore consider it essential always to highlight the greatness of our faith — a commitment from which we must not allow such situations to divert us.[20]

Let's be clear: our popes have not said that abortion, gay marriage, and contraception are morally acceptable or that the

Church should be silent on these matters. In fact, the day after Pope Francis' interview was published, the Holy Father gave a very strong critique of abortion in an address to Catholic gynecologists: Human life "is sacred — at each phase and at every age … it is always valuable. And not as a matter of faith — no, no — but of reason, as a matter of science!" He described abortion as a result of a "widespread mentality of the useful, the 'culture of waste'" that "asks for the elimination of human beings, especially if they are physically or socially weaker. Our response to this mentality is a decisive and unhesitating 'yes' to life."[21]

These are not the words of a man trying to change Catholic teaching on the life issues.

Not the Status Quo

Still, the pope is signaling a new emphasis for the way the Catholic faith should be proclaimed to the world. Given the cultural setting in which we find ourselves, especially in the secular West, we must recognize that we are in mission territory. Tailoring our approach to this reality means that we will focus on the essentials of the Gospel, telling the story of God's love in a way that attracts people, so that their hearts "burn within," as happened when the two disciples encountered Jesus on the road to Emmaus.

> *If you asked the average person, "What does the Catholic Church stand for?" few would say the love and mercy of Jesus Christ.*

Francis' emphasis on God's love and mercy rather than complex moral issues is an important matter of priority and order. "The proclamation of the saving love of God comes before moral and religious imperatives," Francis said in his interview with Fr. Spadaro. "The message of the Gospel, therefore, is not to be reduced to some aspects that, although relevant, on their own do not show the heart of the message of Jesus Christ."

In harmony with previous magisterial teaching, Pope Francis underscores how initial proclamation of the Gospel must come first. Catechesis and then the drawing out of moral consequences for our lives come after, he says. The Gospel message of Christ's love and mercy provides the context for understanding the moral consequences. But without that context (and with the crisis of reason today), how is someone in our secular world to understand why two men can't get married or why a married couple should not use contraception? These are not the ideal lead-off topics for the New Evangelization.

The pope expressed this point best in the interview when discussing how a good homily is structured.

> A beautiful homily, a genuine sermon must begin with the first proclamation, with the proclamation of salvation. There is nothing more solid, deep and sure than this proclamation. Then you have to do catechesis. Then you can draw even a moral consequence. But the proclamation of the saving love of God comes before moral and religious imperatives.... The message of the Gospel, therefore, is not to be reduced to some aspects that, although relevant, on their own do not show the heart of the message of Jesus Christ.

In *The Joy of the Gospel*, Pope Francis elaborates on this. "In today's world of instant communication and occasionally biased media coverage, the message we preach runs a greater risk of being distorted or reduced to some of its secondary aspects" (34). Catholic moral teachings, for example, are often seen not as the pathway to happiness given by the God who loves us, but as rigid rules being imposed on others — the Church telling other people what to do.

Not only are those moral teachings misunderstood, but the very essence of the Catholic faith easily becomes distorted. If, for example, you asked the average person, "What does the Catholic Church stand for?" few would say the love and mercy of Jesus Christ — a love so great that God sent his Son to die for us, to liberate us from our sin and selfishness, and show us the pathway to eternal life. Instead, most would say something like, "The Catholic Church is against abortion," or, "The Church is against ordaining women." That's why Pope Francis concludes, "The biggest problem is when the message we preach then seems identified with those secondary aspects, which, important as they are, do not in and of themselves convey the heart of Christ's message" (EG 34).

We must keep the big picture of the faith in mind and the cultural setting in which we live when we articulate the faith. "We need to be realistic and not assume that our audience understands the full background to what we are saying, or is capable of relating what we say to the very heart of the Gospel which gives it meaning, beauty, and attractiveness" (EG 34).

This approach is in perfect harmony with Pope St. John Paul II, who explained that catechesis is a moment in the larger process of evangelization. It builds upon certain elements of the Church's pastoral mission that prepare for catechesis, including "the initial proclamation of the Gospel or missionary preaching through the *kerygma* to arouse faith" (*Catechesi Tradendae*, 18). It reflects the "divine pedagogy" in which God reveals Himself to humanity gradually and in a proper order, starting with the most fundamental truths of the Gospel that provide the context for expounding on other aspects of the faith. Debating the all-male priesthood or papal infallibility with someone who does not even believe in Jesus Christ, for example, is not likely to bear much fruit. We must address the more fundamental issues first.

The order of the *Catechism of the Catholic Church* also reflects the divine pedagogy.[22] The first pillar of the *Catechism*, the Creed, sums up the story of God's love for us: He created us out of love, sent His Son to die for us out of love, and sent His Spirit into our hearts so that we might participate in His divine love. The second pillar focuses on how we are drawn into that story of God's love through the grace imparted to us in the Sacraments. Then, only after knowing the story of Christ's salvation and after learning how we are filled with Christ's life through the Holy Spirit's work in the liturgy, do we come to the third pillar of the *Catechism*, which addresses the moral life. Here, Christian morality is presented as our response to God's love for us and our life in Christ Jesus. Indeed, the *Catechism* proclaims the Church's moral teachings as a life "worthy of the Gospel," which we are made capable of pursuing by the grace of Christ received in the sacraments and through prayer.

When the Church's moral teachings, however, are taken out of the context of God's loving plan of salvation and our life in Christ, they appear as arbitrary rules from a bygone era being imposed on people today. What is supposed to be the pathway to human beatitude comes off as legalistic moralism. And without the life of sacramental grace — the very grace that makes us capable of living the moral life in Christ — the beautiful moral teachings of the Church can seem quite discouraging. Without grace, people are incapable of pursuing the high call of imitating Christ. People outside the Church, therefore, cannot be asked to practice heroic virtue overnight, and they need much more than a list of strong moral condemnations. They need the initial proclamation of the Gospel to understand the context of the Church's moral teachings. And they need the hope and encouragement that comes with grace, giving us the ability to pursue the good, even when it is difficult to do so.

First Proclamation

As we work in this new kind of missionary territory, we must keep in mind, as noted earlier, that when we share the faith with the baptized, even with those participating in the life of the Church on a regular basis, we cannot assume they have heard the initial proclamation of the Gospel and surrendered their lives to Christ. In the words of Pope Francis, there are some among the baptized "whose lives do not reflect the demands of Baptism, who lack a meaningful relationship to the Church" (EG 14).

Whether we're presenting the faith in parish catechesis, adult faith formation, family ministry, or in the many informal opportunities we encounter in our daily lives, our message must focus on the core elements of the faith, those that have the greatest beauty and appeal and are most essential (EG 35). All the truths of the faith must be believed, but the most essential and compelling dimension of the Catholic faith should always permeate our message: the saving love of God in Jesus Christ:

> All revealed truths derive from the same divine source and are to be believed with the same faith, yet some of them are more important for giving direct expression to the heart of the Gospel. In this basic core, what shines forth is the beauty of the saving love of God made manifest in Jesus Christ who died and rose from the dead. (EG 36)

Christ's saving love is at the center of that first proclamation of the faith, which is meant to attractively invite people to say, "Yes," to Jesus and surrender their lives ever more to him. But Pope Francis emphasizes that this first proclamation is not to be given once, initially, and then brushed aside so that we can move on to deeper theological, moral, and spiritual formation. Rather, the core message of Christ's saving love is fundamental to *all* the Church's activities and must radiate forcefully in all we do:

> On the lips of the catechist the first proclamation must ring out over and over: "Jesus Christ loves you; he gave his life to save you; and now he is living at your side every day to enlighten, strengthen and free you." This first proclamation is called "first" not because it exists at the beginning and can then be forgotten or replaced by other more important things. It is first in a qualitative sense because it is the *principal* proclamation, the one which we must hear again and again in different ways, the one which we must announce one way or another throughout the process of catechesis, at every level and moment. (EG 164)

The Difference between Acts of the Apostles and the Letters of St. Paul

Perhaps the difference between the initial proclamation of the Gospel to which the pope is drawing our attention and the more formal catechesis and moral exhortation that follows can be illustrated by the difference between Acts of the Apostles and the letters of St. Paul. In Acts, the way Peter and Paul initially proclaim the faith to those who have not yet heard the Gospel is different from the way Paul instructs believers in his letters to established Christian communities.

Peter and Paul's initial Gospel presentation in Acts focuses on God's plan of salvation culminating in Jesus Christ dying and rising to save us from our sins. To the crowds at Pentecost, for example, Peter proclaims the core of the Gospel message: Jesus Christ crucified and risen from the dead and the call to repent, be baptized, and be forgiven of sins (Acts 2:14–39). He does the same before the crowds at Solomon's Portico (3:11–26), before the high priest and rulers of Jerusalem (4:8–12), after the angel released him from prison (5:30–32), and when he defends the baptism of the Gentiles (10:34–43).

Paul takes a similar approach, focusing on the core Gospel message on his missionary journeys (Acts 13:16–41; 17:22–31). There is no in-depth challenge on specific moral issues such as infidelity in marriage, neglect of the poor, or unchaste living — not because the people were impeccable in these areas of the moral life, but because they needed the story of salvation before they could comprehend and aspire to live the high moral calling in Christ.[23]

The apostles certainly were not afraid to address tough moral issues. Read Paul's First Letter to the Corinthians, in which he condemns the Christians there for their failure to feed the hungry, their pride, their drunkenness, and their many sexual sins including adultery, prostitution, homosexuality, and incest. But there, Paul was addressing the believers *inside* the Christian community — those who already knew Christ crucified and who surrendered their lives to Him, but were now struggling in their walk with the Lord.

Pope Francis seems to be taking a similar approach. Like Peter and Paul he is more missionary-oriented when he has in mind those outside the Church, leading with dialogue and initial proclamation. But when he addresses those inside the Church, as he did in his 2013 address to Catholic gynecologists, he may focus more clearly on the particular moral consequences of the Christian life.

At the same time, when he draws attention to the core of the Gospel message he speaks volumes to those inside the Church as well. He is reminding us that Catholic identity is not about wearing a badge that says, "I'm pro-life," or, "I don't use contraception," as essential as faithfulness in these moral issues are for Catholic living. The heart of Catholicism is a living encounter with Jesus Christ, intimate communion with the Lord who died for us and wants to forgive us and heal our wounds. That, in fact, is how Pope Francis views his own identity as a Christian. Recall that when asked, "Who is Jorge Mario Bergoglio?" he didn't respond, "I'm a pro-life Catholic," or, "I follow the Church's teachings on human sexuality." Rather, he said he sees himself in the role of Matthew the tax collector, "a sinner on whom the Lord has turned his gaze." I think he is inviting us, when we consider our own identity, to do the same.

Questions for Reflection

1. Pope Francis described the Church as a field hospital. What did he mean by this? If the Church is a field hospital, what aspects of the faith should we focus on when proclaiming it to people who do not yet know the saving love of Christ and are suffering from serious wounds?

2. Pope Francis once said it is not necessary to talk about moral issues such as contraception, gay marriage, and abortion all the time. What did he mean by this? Does this mean the Church's teaching is changing on these moral matters or that we should be silent on these issues? When you are speaking of the faith with skeptics or poorly catechized Catholics, and your listeners challenge you on these and similar points, how do you deal with their questions while at the same time conveying the heart of the Gospel?

3. Pope Francis has said that we must believe all revealed truth, but that some of these truths express the heart of the faith more directly (EG 36). If you had to articulate the heart of the Gospel message, what aspects of the faith would you focus on? What are some examples of secondary aspects of the faith? How might Pope Francis' distinction between "the heart of the Gospel" and "secondary aspects" of the faith shed light on the pope's statement about contraception, abortion, and homosexuality?

4. In presenting the faith, what is the proper relationship between the first proclamation of the Gospel, on one hand, and catechesis and moral teaching, on the other? Which are you more comfortable talking about with others? What can you do to be better at the other?

CHAPTER SIX

WHO AM I TO JUDGE?

Disciples Taking on the Heart of Christ

How do you respond when you happen to notice a person's faults? You witness someone talking too much, losing her temper, criticizing others, or being controlling. You hear of someone living an unchaste life. Or perhaps you know someone who doesn't hold Catholic moral views: he is not pro-life, not for traditional marriage, a relativist at heart and angry with the Church.

In such cases, we can be quick to judge. We say to ourselves, "Oh, she's one of *those* people," "I can't believe a man would do that to his family," or, "What's *her* problem?"

Jesus, however, commands his disciples to take on the compassionate, merciful heart of God: "Be merciful, even as your Father is merciful" (Lk 6:36). Without in any way approving of sinful behavior, Christ's teaching challenges us to examine our hearts: do we have what Pope Francis describes as "an endless desire to show mercy" (EG 24)? Or is our instinct to critique, judge, and condemn? Pope Francis' teachings in *The Joy of the Gospel* challenge us to consider how we view a spouse who hurts us, a child who makes poor decisions, a friend who lets us down, a coworker who makes our life difficult, or flawed leaders in our Church and in our country.

Do we reflect the kind of community whose doors are open to all kinds of people no matter where they may be in their relationship with God? He says he envisions a Church "where there is a place for everyone, with all their problems" — a Church that will "reach everyone without exception or exclusion" (EG 35).

Making Judgments

We may notice that some people have moral issues preventing them from living the Christian life to the full, but Francis reminds us that we may be unaware of the circumstances that have shaped the person's life. We don't know the whole story.

The pope refers to the traditional teaching of the Church that one is morally responsible for his acts to the extent that they are voluntary. Various factors in people's lives may impair their free choices in such a way that limits culpability or moral guilt. He quotes the *Catechism of the Catholic Church* on this point: "*Imputability* and responsibility for an action can be diminished or even nullified by ignorance, inadvertence, duress, fear, habit, inordinate attachments, and other psychological or social factors" (CCC 1735). God sees not just the legal fact of our sins. He also sees our hearts.

> *"Each person's situation before God and their life in grace are mysteries which no one can fully know from without."*
> *— Pope Francis*

A promiscuous female college student who sleeps with one man after another, for example, is doing something that really hurts her and hinders her ability to love and be loved. Her unchaste acts are objectively morally wrong. But if she has never experienced authentic love from her own parents, family, and friends, or has been sexually abused, and she has come to believe that this is the only way she will be valued by others — if she has always been told such behavior is okay, and has never had Catholic teaching on human sexuality explained to her — how culpable is she before God? Only God can tell. Though her promiscuous actions are objectively morally wrong,[24] the extent of her moral responsibility for those actions is not something we can judge from without.[25] Even if she has some degree of culpability, we must remember that the

Lord sees more than the immoral act. He also sees her life situation and interior disposition. He sees her heart.[26]

The Gospel will require us at times to correct others, to teach difficult, challenging truths, and to call people to turn away from objectively evil actions, but Pope Francis says we should always do so "without making judgments about their responsibility and culpability (cf. Mt 7:1; Lk 6:37)." He explains

> "You will never have real mercy for the failings of another until you know and realize that you have the same failings in your soul."
> — St. Bernard of Clairvaux

that "each person's situation before God and their life in grace are mysteries which no one can fully know from without" (EG 172).

Not the Whole Picture

Moreover, we might not be aware of the incremental progress a person may be making in his moral life. We see someone stumble, notice his weakness, and are quick to reach a verdict about his moral character. But we may know nothing of the ways God's grace is moving the person's heart closer to Him. Very small steps for someone suffering from bad habits, hurts, addictions, or dysfunctional patterns of living can be heroic from God's perspective (cf. EG 44). We may not see these small victories, and so instead of celebrating them as gifts of God's grace, we look down upon the person for lacking perfection. That's why St. Thérèse of Lisieux taught that we should always respond to others' faults with charity, "for very often what we think is negligence is heroic in God's eyes. A sister who is suffering from migraine, or is troubled internally, does more when she does half of what is required of her than another who does it all, but is sound in mind and body."[27]

Thérèse herself had great compassion on those in her community who were the hardest to get along with — those who were often angry, jealous, and spiteful, and especially those who had hurt her. Regarding one particular religious sister whose behavior frustrated practically everyone else in the convent, Thérèse said, "I assure you that I have the greatest compassion for Sister X. If you knew her as well as I do, you would see that she is not responsible for all of the things that seem so awful to us. I remind myself that if I had an infirmity such as hers, and so defective a spirit, I would not do any better than she does, and then I would despair; she suffers terribly...."[28] St. Thérèse had a heart full of compassion, not a critical spirit.

The Humility of Fellow Sufferers

Pope Francis says our own personal experience of God and of others being patient with us can teach us much about being compassionate and patient with others (EG 172). Humbly coming to terms with our daily sins and imperfections and experiencing Christ's mercy makes us more merciful toward others and their faults. If we experience God forgiving us and His grace changing our sinful, selfish hearts, we are more likely to respond to others' sins with compassionate understanding rather than judgment. At the core of our being, we know it is God's grace, not our own spiritual talent, that sustains us on the Christian path. As God told St. Catherine of Siena, when we notice someone's faults, we should say to ourselves, "Today it is your turn; tomorrow it will be mine unless divine grace holds me up."[29]

But if, when we notice others' faults, we don't respond with patience and compassion, there may be a serious moral problem *on our end*. If, instead of assuming the best, we find ourselves evaluating and categorizing people — critiquing and judging them — it may be a sign that we do not truly know ourselves and the God who loves us. As St. Bernard of Clairvaux taught, "The sound person feels not the sick one's pains, nor the well-fed the pangs of the hungry. It is fellow sufferers that readily feel compassion for the sick and the hungry.... *You will never have real mercy for the failings of another until you know and realize that you have the same failings in your soul.*"[30]

We might not commit the same outward sinful actions as someone else, but we might struggle with similar root vices in our heart. We might not, for example, fall into adultery, but we may struggle with the lustful thoughts that keep us from giving ourselves as fully as we could to our spouse. We might not be as blatantly vain as others, but we may find ourselves at moments seeking praise and recognition, saddened if we are not at the center of attention, or worried too much about what other people think of us. And we might not have an abortion, but we may shun our responsibility to care for the weakest members of society and thus exhibit the same self-centeredness that contributes to the culture of death.[31] We should let our own experience teach us compassion and patience with others (EG 172).

Following All the Rules

Pope Francis says there's a sense in which a person struggling through moral issues may be in a better spiritual position than the one who outwardly merely follows all the rules. Just because someone appears to be very Catholic from the outside does not mean that he is walking fully in discipleship with the Lord. It does not mean that on the inside he humbly comes before the Lord in his weakness, encounters the mercy of Jesus Christ, and strives to grow in virtue and Christ's love, begging for help all along the way.

A Catholic man may avoid breaking the sixth and ninth commandments concerning adultery and covetousness, for example, but he may still be proud, selfish, and spiritually lazy — complacent with his orthodoxy and mere avoidance of mortal sin. Someone who has struggled for many years to overcome his use of pornography might suddenly find himself encountering the Lord in a more profound way day-to-day, like Matthew the tax collector did, if he sincerely wants to be free of his addictive behavior, lays his sin before Jesus in Confession, decisively turns away from his sin, and begs for Christ's help to keep him on the way of purity. Pope Francis' teaching would suggest that this former addict might now be in a better position spiritually than the man who outwardly appeared to have had his act together all these years, but was not as interested in progressing in the spiritual life.

> A small step, in the midst of great human limitations, can be more pleasing to God than a life which appears outwardly in order but moves through the day without confronting great difficulty. Everyone needs to be touched by the comfort and attraction of God's saving love, which is mysteriously at work in each person, above and beyond their faults and failings (EG 44).

Being a missionary disciple involves confronting our own sins and weaknesses before we think about the problems in other people's lives. And if we truly come to terms with our own failings and encounter Christ's patience and mercy with us, we will be more patient and merciful with others. When we notice their weaknesses, we will be more likely to look "above and beyond their faults" and acknowledge that God's saving love may be "mysteriously at work" in them — because we have experienced his love at work in the midst of our own daily struggles.

"Who Am I to Judge?"

This background can shed light on the comment Pope Francis made about homosexuality to reporters in July 2013. He said, "A gay person who is seeking God, who is of good will — well, who am I to judge him?"

His remarks sparked much controversy, with the media claiming the pope was changing the Church's teachings on homosexuality. In reality, Pope Francis was responding to a reporter's question about the so-called "gay-lobby" that pushes for the Church to change its moral teachings on this matter. When we read the statement in its context, we see that Pope Francis was simply making a distinction between the Church's pastoral approach to homosexuals (which should always be compassionate and welcoming) and its opposition to groups who lobby to change the Church's teachings.

> A gay person who is seeking God, who is of good will — well, who am I to judge him? The *Catechism of the Catholic Church* explains this very well. It says one must not marginalize these persons, they must be integrated into society. The problem isn't this (homosexual) orientation — we must be like brothers and sisters. The problem is something else, the problem is lobbying either for this orientation or a political lobby.[32]

The pope welcomes homosexual persons without in any way endorsing homosexual acts. In fact, he comes right out and rejects efforts made at "lobbying ... for this orientation" and at undermining the Church's moral witness on this issue. At the same time, his comments also underscore the point he emphasizes in *The Joy of the Gospel*: that while we are called to proclaim Christ's teachings and even at times correct others, we must do so without making judgments about how responsible and morally culpable a particular person may be. Instead of judgment, our hearts should be full of mercy and compassion. And we should humbly acknowledge that only the Lord knows "each person's situation before God and their life in grace" (EG 172).

Questions for Reflection

1. Jesus once said, "Be merciful, even as your Father is merciful" (Lk 6:36). How do you typically respond when you notice others' faults, when a colleague frustrates you, or when your spouse hurts you? Do you tend to respond with patience, compassion, and mercy? Or do you tend to respond with judgment and anger? Does your response serve the Gospel or undermine your witness? What might be the ripple effect of your response beyond the immediate situation and even across the years?

2. Reflect on this quote from St. Bernard: "You will never have real mercy for the failings of another until you know and realize that you have the same failings in your soul." Think about someone in your life right now who does not appear to be living a virtuous life or someone whose behavior hurts you. In what ways might this quote from St. Bernard apply to you? In what sense might you have similar failings in your soul? How might your humble experience of God's mercy in your life teach you to be more merciful with others?

3. Pope Francis says there are times when we must teach difficult moral truths, correct others, and even call people to turn away from sinful actions. But we should always do so "without making judgments about their responsibility and culpability." What does he mean by this? Why should we never judge someone's moral responsibility before God when we see them commit objectively immoral acts?

4. Jesus says we should not judge others. Does that mean we should never clearly point out that certain behaviors are right and others are wrong? In Scripture, how do we see Jesus dealing with people who are living morally objectionable lives?

5. What are some of the dangers in making judgments about people's moral character when we happen to notice their faults?

CHAPTER SEVEN

BUILDING A CULTURE OF *ENCUENTRO*

The Crisis of Communal Commitment

Pope Francis is sometimes interpreted only as giving specific political or economic policy advice to world leaders. But at the heart of his message on diverse matters such as globalization, immigration, poverty, and abortion is a personal call to conversion not just for politicians, but for everyone to live less for self and more in solidarity with the human family.

Indeed, he offers a practical message that challenges all of us to examine how we live: How well do we fulfill our responsibilities toward others, whether the people close to us in our families, friendships, workplaces, and parishes or those who need our care in our local communities and the world?

In his 2014 World Day of Peace address, Pope Francis laments the ways the modern world gets us to focus on self and not on the people God has placed in our lives. "New ideologies, characterized by rampant individualism, egocentrism and materialistic consumerism, weaken social bonds," he said. It is as if modern men and women are trained to pursue their own interests — to seek what is beneficial, advantageous, enjoyable, or pleasant for them more than finding their fulfillment in seeking what is best for others, in pursuing a common good.

With this focus on self-interest, our daily relationships tend to be pragmatic and selfish. Christ called us to a sacrificial love that is oriented toward what is best for others. But instead of living out His new commandment, "Love one another as I have loved you," many of our relationships are characterized by a utilitarian attitude that says, "I'll give you this so that you give me that," and "I'll do this for you so that you do this for me." This self-centered spirit leads us to overlook our responsibilities toward others — whether family members, the community, the Church, or the poor.

Our Role in the "Culture of Exclusion"

In *The Joy of the Gospel*, Pope Francis speaks movingly of this crisis of communal commitment when commenting on our indifference toward the needs of the poor.

> To sustain a lifestyle which excludes others, or to sustain enthusiasm for that selfish ideal, a globalization of indifference has developed. Almost without being aware of it, we end up being incapable of feeling compassion at the outcry of the poor, weeping for other people's pain, and feeling a need to help them, *as though all this were someone else's responsibility and not our own.* (EG 54, emphasis added)

Francis is not addressing the problem of poverty itself here. His concerns run much deeper. The root problem is a lack of solidarity with our suffering brethren in the human family. Caught up in our own lives, we fail to care for others and in some cases are not even aware of their existence or their needs as fellow human persons. Busy pursuing our own careers, wealth, possessions, and dreams of "financial security," we don't even notice that many people around us are barely surviving day-to-day.

The pope asks why a decline in the stock market captures our attention, but the death of a homeless person on the street, in the cold, does not. We remain unmoved by human suffering, deadened by our fixation on prosperity (EG 53, 54).

This pervasive indifference exemplifies what Pope Francis calls the "culture of exclusion." Countless human beings among us are not even taken into consideration as a part of society. They are completely overlooked. "It's no longer simply about exploitation and oppression.... Those excluded are no longer society's underside or its fringes or its disenfranchised — they are no longer even a part of it. The excluded are not the 'exploited' but the outcast, the 'leftovers'" (EG 53).

To overcome the culture of exclusion Pope Francis calls us to build a "culture of encounter" — a culture in which we get out of ourselves and have personal contact with the people around us, really looking at them, listening to them and treating them as true brothers and sisters. He illustrated this vision of encounter poignantly in a 2013 address to pilgrims in Buenos Aires in which he challenges us to give something much more valuable than money to the poor. He challenges us to give of ourselves.

> I sometimes ask people: "Do you give alms?" They say
> to me: "Yes, Father." "And when you give alms, do you
> look the person you are giving them to in the eye?" "Oh,
> I don't know, I don't really notice." "Then you have not
> really encountered him. You tossed him the alms and
> walked off. When you give alms, do you touch the per-
> son's hand or do you throw the coin?" "No, I throw the
> coin." "So you did not touch him. And if you don't touch
> him you don't meet him."[33]

These words about the poor can be applied to all of our relationships. Pope Francis challenges us to have a true "encounter" — *encuentro* in Spanish — with the people who are part of our daily lives. Do I know what is going on in the lives of the people in my office? Do I take time to truly share life with my children? Do I know what is weighing on my spouse's heart? As relational beings, all persons long for someone to walk beside them, to share the joys and sorrows, dreams and fears, triumphs and hardships that make up life. But today, there is a "profound *poverty of relationships*," as Pope Francis said in his message on the

2014 World Day of Peace (5). We are too busy pursuing our own projects and entertaining ourselves on screens to see the real faces of the people in our lives.

Instead of personal encounter — a true sharing of life together — most of our interactions are reduced to getting the information we need from a coworker, updating our boss on our projects, successfully getting the kids to pick up their toys, and texting our spouse about what time we will be home. There is much communication between people in this flurry of activity, but little *communio*, few opportunities to "encounter" each other personally.

A Deeper Poverty

This is why Blessed Mother Teresa said that some of the greatest poverty in the world is in the prosperous West. It is not a material poverty, but a deeper one — a poverty of friendship, love, and care. Her Missionary of Charity sisters often describe how it is much harder to serve the poor in the United States, for example, than the poor in India. One sister in Calcutta told me, "With the poor here in India, we can help satisfy their hunger. We can give them food. But many people in the United States have a hunger that is not as easy to fill: they hunger for love — the love of their parents, their brother or sister, their spouse."

Mother Teresa once described this kind of poverty of relationships when she visited a nursing home where children send their elderly parents.

> I saw in that home they had everything, beautiful things, but everybody was looking towards the door. And I did not see a single one with their smile on their face. And I turned to the Sister and I asked: How is that? How is it that the people they have everything here, why are they all looking towards the door, why are they not smiling?... And she said: This is nearly every day, they are expecting, they are hoping that a son or daughter will come to visit them. They are hurt because they are forgotten.[34]

We don't have to turn far to encounter the poor: "That poverty comes right there in our own home, even neglect to love. Maybe in our own family we have somebody who is feeling lonely, who is feeling sick, who is feeling worried, and these are difficult days for everybody. Are we there, are we there to receive them?"[35] That's why Mother Teresa often said, "Never worry about numbers. Help one person at a time and always start with the person nearest you."[36]

Social Media

The Holy Father's call to build a culture of *encuentro* challenges us to consider the impact of technology and social media on our ability to give the best of ourselves to the people around us. Pope Francis is particularly concerned that in our hyper-connected world we often interact with screens more than with people. In *The Joy of the Gospel*, he quotes Pope Paul VI's observation that "technological society has succeeded in multiplying occasions of pleasure, yet has found it very difficult to engender joy."[37]

This modern inward turn leaves us, like Matthew's friends in the tax collector's office, looking down — not at our money, but at our mobile devices, trapped in self-interest.

How often does your smart phone, for example, interrupt conversation with your family, friends, or colleagues? And how much does the time spent communicating on screens prevent you from giving the best of yourself to the people around you? The pope particularly challenges those who like to hide behind technology for communication rather than converse in a more personal manner with others — "those who want their interpersonal relationships provided by sophisticated equipment, by screens and systems which can be turned on and off on command" (EG 88).

Text messaging and social media, for example, give us a sense of control in our interactions with others. We can have time to process how to respond to someone, shape our message, and project a certain image of ourselves. We also can protect ourselves from awkward moments or conflict with others. But to truly encounter another person, we can't turn them on and off "on command." And we can't hide behind screens. We must walk with them closely in real time. "The Gospel tells us constantly to run the risk of a face-to-face encounter with others," Pope Francis says, "with their physical presence, which challenges us, with their pain and their pleas, with their joy, which infects us in our close and continuous interaction" (EG 88).

Encuentro at Home

Pope Francis' call for *encuentro* also challenges parents to think about how they interact with their own children. I've heard many fathers admit that sometimes they come home from work and relate to their children more like a military captain marshaling the troops to finish their homework, practice their music, pick up their toys, get their pajamas on, brush their teeth, and get to bed on time. When I fall into a "get-it-done" mode like this, I might successfully get the kids to accomplish their evening responsibilities, but I have to ask myself, "Am I any closer to them at the end of the night?" There may be plenty of interaction, but if there is not a true sharing of life, not much *encuentro*, we end up relating to our children more like Captain von Trapp from *The Sound of Music* than a father who is personally involved in their lives.

> *"Be very close to your children.... They need you, your presence, to be there, your love!"*
> — *Pope Francis*

Pope Francis' teaching challenges all parents to make sure we are not just giving our children a good house, a good education, and good activities, but even more, that we are giving *ourselves* to them — truly *encountering* them personally day-to-day. In a world where fathers often don't give the best of themselves to their children because they are too busy pouring their lives into their work and career, Pope Francis challenges them to "waste time" with their children.[38] His message to fathers on the Solemnity of St. Joseph makes a similar point — one that can be applied to mothers just as well — "Be very close to your children.... They need you, your presence, to be there, your love!"[39]

The pope's message also challenges us to examine our marriages. Do we truly encounter our spouse day-to-day? Do we take time to know what is really going on in his or her heart? I wrote this chapter on encounter the week after my wife gave birth to our seventh child. I took several days off of work to be at home and help manage the household while my wife was resting in bed and taking care of our newborn. Having to handle all the responsibilities at home made me appreciate even more all that my wife does for our family! I did the cooking and the laundry and took care of the children, driving them to their various music lessons and practices so that my wife could recover and focus on the baby. I brought meals to her, went to the store for her, brought her medicines, filled her water bottle, brought her the mail — basically, I tried to respond to whatever needs or requests she had.

In those busy days, I initially thought I was serving my wife well. But one night, when the kids were down and I was writing this very chapter about *encuentro*, Pope Francis' words made me realize how much I was falling short of the mark. I could write about *encuentro*, but I wasn't living it as well as I should! It hit me when I brought Beth some food, asked her how she was doing, and she said, "I'm lonely." My wife needed more than food, drink, laundry, flowers, medicine, and baby diapers. She needed me. She just needed some adult conversation and time to connect with her husband. This was a wake-up call for me. I don't want to simply rush around providing acts of service for my wife; I also want to take time for that personal connection with her.

Many things can get in the way of that connection in a marriage, whether problems with a child, financial troubles, health issues, an unresolved conflict in the marriage relationship, pressures at work, or the hectic weeks after welcoming a newborn. But even amid the trials of life, spouses must remember they are not coworkers tackling projects and problems together. They are two who have become one in Christ, and they need to regularly take time for the personal encounter with each other that deepens that unity.

Pope Francis calls us to build a culture of encounter in our daily lives, but we must do this intentionally: "What Jesus teaches us first of all is to meet each other, and in meeting to offer each other help. We must know how to meet each other. We must build, create, construct a culture of encounter. How many differences, how many problems in the family there always are! Problems in the neighborhood, problems at work, problems everywhere," he said. We need to build "the culture of encounter," which is simply about taking time to go out of ourselves and truly "meet" the other person.[40]

Questions for Reflection

1. How much do you sense responsibility to care for the poor and suffering in the world? In what ways might you contribute to the "culture of exclusion"?

2. Pope Francis is concerned not only about material poverty, but also what he calls a "poverty of relationships." What does he mean by this? Do you see this kind of poverty in our own country? Have *you* ever experienced this type of poverty?

3. In response to this poverty of relationships, Pope Francis calls us to build a "culture of encounter" — an environment in which we walk among others in life, truly sharing life with them, sharing in the joys, sorrows, dreams, and fears of the people around us. How is this culture of encounter different from the way most people interact with each other today?

4. Consider the people you interact with on a regular basis — your spouse, children, coworkers, friends, and neighbors. How well do you know what is going on in their lives, what is weighing on their hearts? Pick one or two of these relationships and consider what you can do practically to encounter them more as persons and live more in solidarity with them day-to-day.

CHAPTER EIGHT

THE FIVE TEMPTATIONS OF MISSIONARY DISCIPLES

Motivated By Mission or Self-Interest?

Imagine if Pope Francis came to your parish to visit the pastor, staff, volunteers, and you, and he opened up about his own spiritual life, admitting that that he sometimes struggles with selfishness in his work in the Church and that he wishes he were more generous in his service to Christ.

Such a scene would be quite moving! If the Holy Father humbly acknowledged that *he* struggles with selfishness and wishes that *he* gave more of his life in service to God, surely that would make us re-evaluate our own lives: Am *I* giving the best of myself in service to the Church? How much does selfishness keep *me* from giving more of my life to Christ?

That's basically what Pope Francis has done in the middle of chapter three of *The Joy of the Gospel*. After praising the pastoral workers around the world who joyfully sacrifice their lives and their time, he said, "This witness comforts and sustains me in my own effort to overcome selfishness and give more fully of myself" (EG 76).

This is a key turning point in the whole document. In the first half of chapter three, Pope Francis critiqued the self-centered individualism that is so pervasive in our world today. Now in the second half of chapter three, he turns his attention to the Church and challenges us to examine how much this individualistic mentality affects our apostolic work. "As children of this age … all of us are in some way affected by the present globalized culture" (EG 77).

People working in various pastoral settings have told me that this is the section of *The Joy of the Gospel* they find most personally challenging. It's like an examination of conscience, calling us to honestly ask ourselves, "How much have the world's ways affected my work in the Church?" "How much am I really motivated by mission, driven to give myself generously to whatever is good for the Church and for the people I serve? And how much

> *Instead of seriously considering new approaches and opportunities to share the Gospel, we say, "We'll take that idea to the next committee meeting."*

am I motivated by self-interest — by pursuit of what is comfortable, easy, and beneficial for me, my reputation, and my career?"

Pope Francis lists several key temptations missionary disciples, especially those working in the Church, might face.

1. Identity Crisis — Mission or Just Work?

Pope Francis is concerned that the self-centered spirit of our day is not just a problem out in the world; it's a problem within the Church. The same individualistic mentality that fosters moral relativism, neglect of the poor, abortion, and the breakdown of marriage and family life also can prevent pastoral workers in the Church from giving themselves more fully to the work of evangelization.

This happens when certain catechists, teachers, youth ministers, or clergy view their apostolic work more as a job than a life-shaping mission. What may have started as a burning desire to bring the love of Christ to souls who don't know him gradually succumbs to concerns over freedom, comfort, reputation, career, and financial gain. Self-interest, not souls, keeps these workers awake at night. Instead of being "on the lookout" for opportunities to share the Gospel,[41] they are on the lookout for opportunities for themselves.

We have already seen that such pastoral workers are not as likely to take on new initiatives that might further evangelization and even less likely to "go out" and personally encounter those who need the joy of the Gospel. Pope Francis points out that too often lay people are afraid they'll be asked to take on a project that will cut into their free time. And he says some priests are more "obsessed with protecting their free time" than they are driven to give themselves over completely to the mission of evangelization. "This is frequently due to the fact that people feel an overbearing need to guard their personal freedom, as though the task of evangelization was a dangerous poison rather than a joyful response to God's love which summons us to mission and makes us fulfilled and productive" (EG 81). Instead of seriously considering new approaches and opportunities to share the Gospel, we say, "We'll take that idea to the next committee meeting," or, "We'll have to see how that fits into the budget." Or, like my beloved Chicago Cubs, who always seem very comfortable with mediocre, we say at the outset, "Maybe next year."

Certainly, we must be careful in balancing our lives well, ensuring time for prayer, friendship, family, and leisure. There are plenty of pastoral workers who have fallen into over-activity that leads to burnout. Still, Pope Francis challenges all of us, even the busiest, to honestly examine what really motivates the decisions we make in pastoral ministry — how we spend our time, how we spend our money, what initiatives we pursue, and which ones we choose not to do.

Some pastoral settings have leaders "acting as if God did not exist," Francis says, "making decisions as if the poor did not exist, setting goals as if others did not exist, working as if people who have not received the Gospel did not exist." He notes that leaders who have solid doctrinal and spiritual beliefs are not exempt from this temptation and can fall into a self-serving lifestyle that focuses on personal gain and "leads to an attachment to financial security, or to a desire for power or human glory at all cost, rather than giving their lives to others in mission" (EG 80).

At the heart of this issue is a crisis of identity: Do we view mission as at the core of our being or do we view apostolic work as something extra, a noble job but one that sometimes interferes with our personal life? "Today we are seeing in many pastoral workers ... an inordinate concern for their personal freedom and relaxation, which leads them to see their work as a mere appendage to their life, as if it were not part of their very identity" (EG 78). When mission fails to shape their lives and apostolic work is just a job, pastoral workers are unable to give themselves fully to the New Evangelization. "As a result, one can observe in many agents of evangelization, even though they pray, a heightened individualism, a crisis of identity, and a cooling of fervor. These are three evils which fuel one another" (EG 79).

2. Pastoral Sloth — "The Gray Pragmatism of the Daily Life of the Church"

Acedia — commonly translated as *sloth* — is not simply laziness, though that may be one sign of the vice. In the Catholic tradition, sloth is seen as the sorrow one has toward all that friendship with God entails. We are made to rest in God, but the demands of God's love are too great. The call to die to self is seen as too burdensome. The slothful soul shrinks from the spiritual effort and self-sacrifice that a relationship with God requires. Like the Rich Young Man, one turns away sadly from the invitation to follow Christ completely.

Pope Francis notes that when pastoral workers see their work more as a job than a life-shaping mission, they wind up feeling paralyzed and succumbing to acedia.

One Biblical analogy sometimes used to depict the vice of acedia is Israel's desert wanderings. God's people were offered the opportunity to enter the Promised Land one year after their liberation from Egypt. But when they realized the effort and struggle that settling the land would entail, they rebelled, refused God's gift, and were condemned to wander through the wilderness for forty years (Numbers 13–14). Instead of finding joy and rest in the Promised Land, the people of Israel, weary and restless, unsure where they were going next and often grumbling, wandered in circles in the desert.

> *"Deep down, we know what we're doing is not really working, but we keep doing it year after year."*

That image of Israel roaming in the wilderness describes how some pastoral workers in parishes and dioceses feel: weary, aimless, restless, and unsure about why they are doing what they are doing. "We often feel like we're just spinning our wheels," one former diocesan leader told me. "Deep down, we know what we're doing is not really working, but we keep doing it year after year." Another wondered, "We say we're very busy, but are we really busy pursuing the Church's mission or are we just weighed down by busywork?"

Similarly, a parish director of religious education admitted: "I often wonder who I'm doing all this for. Is it really for Christ? Is it really about mission? Or is it just because we're reacting to some small group in the parish or because the pastor is mad about something or because some mandate came down from the diocese?"

Vividly expressing this point, one diocesan leader said some chancery offices feel more like the DMV than a warm, joyful, welcoming community united in a thrilling, common mission. Though there are always some enthusiastic workers, he noted how other staff simply clock in and clock out, are not excited to be there, and do not find much joy in their work. They view visitors coming in with requests not as souls to serve but as more work for them to do. Hence the "take a number" ambiance some people experience. "We're supposed to be partners with the pastors and the parishes and working to assist the bishop. But in this environment, we can easily forget that we're serving the Lord, the Church, the bishop, and the parishes," he said.

Pope Francis is concerned about what he calls "pastoral acedia" — a sloth that may underlie a fury of busyness. He addresses the problem of pastoral work "undertaken badly, without adequate motivation, without a spirituality which would permeate it and make it pleasurable. As a result, work becomes more tiring than necessary.... Far from a content and happy tiredness, this is a tense, burdensome, dissatisfying, and, in the end, unbearable fatigue" (EG 82).

What causes pastoral acedia? The pope gives several reasons. Sometimes we throw ourselves into unrealistic projects, setting the bar too high when we should be content to do less, but do it very well. Sometimes we lack patience, expecting a big impact right away as opposed to planting the small mustard seed and caring for it so that it grows.

Some of us might be too attached to certain pet projects that prevent us from being open to other avenues of evangelization. Others give ourselves to planning and organizing but lose contact with real people so that our decisions are out of touch with their needs.

But one of the most challenging lines from this section of *The Joy of the Gospel* comes when Francis describes how it can be very difficult for pastoral workers "to tolerate anything that smacks of disagreement, possible failure, criticism, the cross" (EG 82). Let's break down those four points.

Fear of disagreement: We might shrink from serving the Church in important ways because we are too afraid to disagree with our boss or pastor. Our superior, for example, wants to do something that we know is not a good idea, but we want to stay on his or her good side. It's easier to stay quiet than to risk conflict, even though we can see problems unfolding ahead. Or maybe we don't want to disagree with a strong-willed coworker because it will require too much effort to convince the person. Or perhaps there are "turf wars" and we are just afraid of upsetting someone in another department. Instead of helping our colleagues for the good of the Church, we just go on minding our own business, never bringing up difficult situations while we go back to our silos saying to ourselves, "This is going to be a train wreck."

While we should always be prudent and charitable in how we address disagreements, fear of conflict causes an array of dysfunction in any organization. In pastoral work, it hinders the Church in its evangelizing mission and prevents us from contributing the best we can to serve souls.

Fear of Failure: Another weakness that keeps us from giving the best of ourselves to the Church's mission is fear of failure. Some pastoral workers sincerely want to do good for the Church but they fear letting down their bishop or pastor to such an extent that they shrink from new challenges and opportunities. Others fear failure for less noble reasons: they're afraid of what others may think of them and afraid of how a mistake might affect their careers. Concerned about impressing a boss, exciting a crowd, and moving up the ladder, they dread taking on new kinds of initiatives in which they may not shine as well.

> *We find ourselves tailoring much of our work just to keep a small group of people happy rather than reaching out to those many souls who don't know friendship with Jesus Christ.*

In either case, we tend to avoid apostolic endeavors that throw us out of our comfort zones. We might focus on the risks and weaknesses of these new approaches and even openly criticize them — not because they're bad, but because we want to excuse ourselves from having to try them, even though they might be good for the Church and good for our own professional and spiritual development.

Fear of Criticism: A third defect that hinders our pastoral work is fear of criticism. Especially in parish life, there can be a lot of murmuring. We can be afraid of what some groups or certain individuals in the parish may think of us, especially donors and others who have the pastor's ear. So we find ourselves tailoring much of our work just to keep a small group of people happy rather than reaching out to those many souls who don't know friendship with Jesus Christ.

Moreover, this "inner circle" of parish life — those who are most influential and most involved — typically does not like change. That's why they keep coming to everything at the parish. For the most part, they're content with the status quo. That's why new parish leaders — whether clergy, religious, or laity — who come in with grand ideas for adult faith formation and evangelization quickly become disillusioned. If someone changes the time or location for a group's meeting, it might spark World War III ("We've met at this time for fourteen years!"). Starting a dramatically new kind of initiative, challenging people to "go out," or changing the way the parish operates seems almost completely out of the question. Of course, moving a parish to a more outward focus takes prudence, charity, and a lot of patience, but when we become enslaved to fear of criticism, we can't even get the ship heading in the right direction.

Finally, we must remember there will always be grumbling and criticism. The question is, what will we do when the criticism comes? St. Josemaría Escrivá once said, "Don't waste your time and your energy — which belong to God — throwing stones at the dogs that bark at you on your way." There will always be barking dogs. Sometimes you just have to move ahead without trying to placate every one of them.

Fear of the Cross: Ultimately, each of the previous three fears — fear of disagreement, failure, and criticism — stem from fear of the cross. Being a disciple of Christ involves picking up our cross and following him. We will, therefore, be misunderstood and mistreated if we truly follow Christ. We shouldn't seek out conflict and criticism, but we should not shy away from it when it comes.

When pastoral workers, however, are slavishly worried about protecting their reputation, career, or "good standing," they will find themselves paralyzed. They'll be stuck in the grim reality of communal dysfunction and the rut of using the same approaches, programs, and organizations that do not effectively draw outsiders in. Afraid of the cross, we tend to avoid doing anything that might veer from the safer, mainstream ways of doing things. And Pope Francis said this is the biggest danger of all: "The gray pragmatism of the daily life of the Church, in which all appears to proceed normally, while in reality faith is wearing down and degenerating into small-mindedness" (EG 83).

3. Sterile Pessimism: A Self-Centered Lack of Trust

Pope Francis has a sober understanding of the serious troubles facing our world today. Earlier in chapter three of *The Joy of the Gospel*, he warned that humanity is experiencing "a turning point in its history" (EG 52). Throughout this opening section on "Some Challenges of Today's World" (EG 52–75), he weighs seriously the epochal changes the human family faces in an array of areas — poverty, isolation, global economic structures, consumerism, the instant impact of the media, relativism, secularism, and the breakdown of marriage, family, and personal relationships. He paints a stark picture of where humanity is heading and concludes that these present realties, unless effectively addressed, could unleash a dehumanizing process that it would be difficult to halt (EG 51).

But he also approaches these challenges full of hope — trusting in the God who can bring life out of death, and light from the darkness. He says the evils of the world should never take away our joy in the Gospel and our confidence in the Lord. "We are distressed by the troubles of our age ... yet the fact that we are more realistic must not mean that we are any less trusting in the Spirit or less generous" (EG 84). He quotes the famous words of St. John XIII from the opening of the Second Vatican Council:

> At times we have to listen, much to our regret, to the voices of people who, though burning with zeal, lack a sense of discretion and measure. In this modern age they can see nothing but prevarication and ruin.... We feel that we must disagree with those prophets of doom who are always forecasting disaster, as though the end of the world were at hand. In our times, divine Providence is leading us to a new order of human relations, which, by human effort and even beyond all expectations, are directed to

the fulfillment of God's superior and inscrutable designs, in which everything, even human setbacks, leads to the greater good of the Church.[42]

The central issue at stake here is hope. Defeatism is a great temptation, hindering our ability to give ourselves to evangelization, and turning us into what Pope Francis calls "querulous and disillusioned pessimists, 'sourpusses'" (EG 85). Like the despairing Lord Denathor of Gondor in J.R.R. Tolkein's *The Lord of the Rings*, we can be tempted to see only the evils of the world, viewing the challenges from our limited human perspective. Without hope in God — trusting in his providence and his grace — we will fall into discouragement or even despair over what, from human eyes, seem to be insurmountable obstacles. And we will be tempted to use that defeatist perspective — and here's the key — to excuse ourselves from going out to meet others with zeal for evangelization. We will use our pessimism to justify our less than joyful, sacrificial generosity in serving Christ, and our tendency to look down upon those who enthusiastically throw themselves, from our point of view *naively*, into joyful evangelization.

When cynical pessimism creeps into our hearts, we might say to ourselves, "Why bother?" Pope Francis challenges those of us who fall into this kind of discouragement to get out of ourselves: "Nobody can go off to battle unless he is fully convinced of victory beforehand. If we start without confidence, we have already lost half the battle and we bury our talents" (EG 85). We mustn't give in to anxiety and the refusal to trust. "The evils of our world ... must not be excuses for diminishing our commitment and our fervor" (EG 84).

Christians should refuse to work from the perspective of defeat (EG 96). To do so is to "deny our history as a Church, which is glorious precisely because it is a history of sacrifice, of hopes, and daily struggles, of lives spent in service ..." (EG 96). Think of the heroism of the saints throughout the Church's history who strove against all odds, confidently fought for souls, and boldly proclaimed the Gospel in the midst of dire circumstances such as persecutions in the early Church or the horrors of the Holocaust. They all trusted in a God whom they believed could work miracles, even bringing good out of evil. Some persevered in their witness to the point of martyrdom. St. Ignatius of Antioch or St. Maximilian Kolbe, for example, were not defeatist generals or cynical sourpusses. They exemplified a heroic witness full of joy and hope amid far greater adversities than most of us face today.

A hope-filled evangelizer believes that even in the desert of modern secularism, people are still thirsting. Francis quotes Pope Benedict XVI, who noted that "… in today's world there are innumerable signs, often expressed implicitly or negatively, of the thirst for God, for the ultimate meaning of life. And in the desert people of faith are needed who, by the example of their own lives, point out the way to the Promised Land and keep hope alive" (EG 86). Francis goes on to say,

> Today, our challenge is not so much atheism as the need to respond adequately to many people's thirst for God, lest they try to satisfy it with alienating solutions…. Unless these people find in the church a spirituality which can offer healing and liberation … they will end up by being taken in by solutions which neither make life truly human nor give glory to God. (EG 89)

4. Spiritual Worldliness

Spiritual worldliness is another hindrance to evangelization that can sneak into the hearts of pastoral workers. The signs of this defect are harder to detect because from the outside, the person appears to be very pious and full of love for the Church. But underneath these appearances, which are often carefully cultivated, the spiritually worldly person seeks his own glory, pleasure, and personal well-being, not Christ's interests.

Pope Francis says there are two main causes of spiritual worldliness. One he depicts as gnosticism — a purely subjective faith interested only in a set of ideas or spiritual experiences. For example, someone might enjoy thinking and talking about certain ideas, a favorite philosopher or theologian, a particular doctrinal point, levels of mysticism, and so forth. Another person might derive much enjoyment from certain spiritual practices and experiences, whether through private devotions, or particular kinds of music, or the smells and bells of the liturgy. God can use these to bring enlightenment and consolation to the soul, but when these ideas and experiences themselves become primary, they can effectively trap people in their own emotions or ideas (EG 94). The person becomes more concerned with the enjoyment they derive from them than about serving God Himself. Caught up in themselves, they show little concern for others.

A second cause of spiritual worldliness is what Pope Francis calls "self-absorbed promethean neopelagianism." Now that's a mouthful! What does he mean? In Greek mythology, Prometheus was the Titan who defied the gods and created man and fire. He is an image of human striving. Pelagianism is the belief that human nature was not tainted by original sin. In this view, we don't need God's grace to help us to do good, we can do it all by our own effort. Pope Francis has in mind Christians who, trusting solely in themselves, fail to acknowledge how radically dependent they are on God — how, in the words of St. Thérèse of Lisieux, "all is grace." The great danger is that when we attempt to be superhero Christians, we might be tempted to look down on others because we "observe certain rules" or follow a particular style of Catholicism that others don't.

> A supposed soundness of doctrine or discipline leads instead to a narcissistic and authoritarian elitism, whereby instead of evangelizing, one analyzes and classifies others, and instead of opening the door to grace, one exhausts his or her energies in inspecting and verifying. (EG 94)

Like a good doctor, Francis lists several possible symptoms of spiritual worldliness. Some who suffer from this illness are brazenly preoccupied with safeguarding the liturgy and doctrine but show little concern for the actual impact of the Gospel on people and on contemporary needs and challenges (EG 95). Others are fascinated with appearing important, enjoying a social life with high-profile meetings, dinners, banquets, and receptions. Others pride themselves on their administrative skills, developing plans with objectives, statistics, management strategies, and evaluation processes but without going out of themselves much to personally connect with those who don't know the Gospel. A common denominator with all these symptoms of spiritual worldliness is a lack of an outward focus, a failure to search out those who hunger for Christ, a self-indulgent complacency in place of a fervent evangelical spirit (EG 95).

One of the effects of spiritual worldliness is that these pastoral workers become detached from real people and their needs. "We waste time talking about 'what needs to be done' ... like spiritual masters and pastoral experts who give instructions from on high. We indulge in endless fantasies and we lose contact with the real lives and difficulties of our people" (EG 96).

Closed to new ideas, spiritually-worldly pastoral workers tend to "reject the prophecy of their brothers and sisters" and discredit anyone who raises questions about how things are currently being done (EG 97). They also let their idealism hinder new opportunities for the Church's growth, allowing the perfect to stand in the way of doing good. They remain aloof as pastoral, catechetical, or liturgical purists, and "constantly point out the mistakes of others" instead of proposing new approaches or actually getting into the trenches themselves to evangelize (EG 97).

Pope Francis says this spiritual worldliness in the Church is "a tremendous corruption disguised as good," and "self-centeredness cloaked in an outward religiosity bereft of God" (EG 97). He offers three basic ways for the Church to avoid it:

- The Church must constantly go out of herself and not fall into ecclesial introspection.

- The Church must keep its mission focused on Jesus Christ, each person maintaining a personal encounter with Christ day-to-day and sharing the joy of Christ with others.

- And, finally, the Church must always maintain its commitment to serving Christ in the poor.

5. Workers in the Vineyard at War
with One Other

On the night before he died, Jesus prayed to the Father that all Christians would be one and that this witness of Christian unity would be a source of inspiration for others to come to faith. Jesus prayed "that they may all be one; even as you, Father, are in me, and I in you, that they also may be in us, so that the world may believe that you have sent me" (John 17:21).

But when believers who are supposed to be working together in Christ's Church are at war with each other, what kind of message does this send? Pope Francis laments the scandalous divisions among pastoral workers and members of religious communities who are caught up in petty battles with each other over control, power moves, and reputation rather than standing shoulder-to-shoulder together in the good fight for evangelization. Spiritual worldliness leads some pastoral workers to fight against others "who stand in the way of their quest for power, prestige, pleasure and economic security." Others may fall into a kind of exclusivity, priding themselves on being a part of a certain group or movement that they think puts them into an elite class of Catholicism. "Instead of belonging to the whole Church in all its rich variety, they belong to this or that group which thinks itself different and special" (EG 98).

In the face of the pervasive individualism of our age that divides the human family, witness of Christian community needs to shine even more brightly. "I especially ask Christians in communities throughout the world to offer a radiant and attractive witness of fraternal communion. Let everyone admire how you care for one another, and how you encourage and accompany one another" (EG 99). We can draw several practical challenges from this section of *The Joy of the Gospel*:

- In a world characterized by the pursuit of self-interest, let our parishes, chancery offices, and religious communities be a living witness to what Pope Francis calls "a mystical fraternity" — a love capable of "seeing the sacred grandeur of our neighbor, of finding God in every human being" (EG 92).

- In a world in which people avoid others who are unpleasant and difficult to deal with, let us bear witness to a love that tolerates, through God's love, the annoyances and inconveniences of daily life — especially in our own families, offices, parishes, and religious communities (EG 92).

- In a world that encourages us to view our relationships primarily in terms of what we get out of them, let us bear witness to a selfless, sacrificial love that seeks what is best for others before our own interests.

- In a world plagued by rivalries, jealousies, and a desire for praise and attention, let us rejoice in the gifts and accomplishments of our fellow laborers in the vineyard, remembering "we are all in the same boat and headed to the same port" and that the gifts of any individual benefit the whole community (EG 99).

- In a world in which many people are divided by years of anger and resentment, let us bear witness to a love that prays for those who hurt us — whether it be a relative, coworker, boss, or pastor. It is a beautiful thing, the pope tells us, to hold in prayer a person who irritates us, and to do so is actually a step forward in evangelization (EG 101).

All in all, Pope Francis calls us to model a way of living together that is foreign to our individualistic world and gives radiant witness to the love of Jesus Christ shining through our communities. As salt and light, "we are called to bear witness to a constantly new way of living together in fidelity to the Gospel. Let us not allow ourselves to be robbed of community!" (EG 92).

Questions for Reflection

1. *Mission or Just Work?* In whatever work you may do for the Church (whether as a pastoral worker, volunteer, or

participant), do you make decisions based more on what will best serve the Church's mission or on your own interests — what is easier, more comfortable, more advantageous for your career, or more financially beneficial *for you*?

2. *Pastoral Sloth:* How much do you allow fear of more work, fear of failure, or fear of conflict keep you from trying new ideas and giving the best of yourself to the Church's mission? How does this same dynamic affect your relationships with family members or friends?

3. *Sterile Pessimism:* How confidently do you face the challenges that come up in the work of evangelization? Do you get easily discouraged by the direction the world is going and the human weaknesses in the Church? How much do you trust that God can work through the greatest trials to bring good even in the midst of great darkness?

4. *Spiritual Worldliness:* Are you more concerned about going out and serving others, or are you more motivated to seek certain spiritual experiences or think and talk about your favorite Catholic topics? Do you find yourself looking down on others who don't hold to certain ideas or follow a set of rules that you do? Are you anxious to be invited to important meetings and receptions? Do you seek your security in being a good administrator rather than being with the people — in being a CEO more than a shepherd?

5. *Workers at War with Each Other:* In your work in the Church — whether as an employee or as a volunteer — what shapes your decisions more: a concern to maintain control and power or a humble willingness to let others influence the direction of your parish/diocese/community for the good of the Church? Are you envious of other pastoral workers or do you thank God for the ways their gifts build up the Body of Christ? Do you pray and lovingly offer sacrifices for coworkers who hurt you or do you allow resentment and division to fester in your heart?

CHAPTER NINE

PROCLAIMING THE FAITH TODAY

The Art of Preaching and Teaching

In the section of *The Joy of the Gospel* devoted to preaching (135–159), Pope Francis' reflections focus mostly on clergy giving homilies. But his insights about the art of communicating the faith are applicable to a wide range of settings. Anyone teaching the faith — whether it be catechists, Bible study leaders, youth ministers, school teachers, or parents teaching their children — will benefit from his guidance in this section.

Between the Two Embraces

The word *homily* is Greek for "explanation." In the Mass, it is an explanation of the Word of God proclaimed in the liturgy. The homily is so important for passing on the faith that Vatican Council II stated it should hold "pride of place" among the various forms of Christian instruction.[43] This is so, Pope Francis says, because of its Eucharistic context: the homily "is the supreme moment in the dialogue between God and his people which leads up to sacramental communion" (EG 137).

The key word here is dialogue. The homily is not an ordinary explanation like one found in the encyclopedia. It is not merely an intellectual enterprise in which important images and ideas in the Scriptures are clarified. Any explanation given is at the service of the dialogue *already* taking place between God and His people. The preacher is not getting on stage to captivate our attention, share his wisdom, and offer practical advice for life. Rather, he's stepping into a conversation that has already started. His role is simply to help further that conversation.

Pope Francis says the preacher is an intermediary who has the challenging but beautiful mission of uniting the heart of God and the hearts of his people. "The Lord and his people speak to one another in a thousand ways directly, without intermediaries. But in the homily they want someone to serve as an instrument and to express their feelings in such a way that afterward, each one may choose how he or she will continue the conversation" (EG 143).

In one of his most beautiful images, Pope Francis describes the task of the preacher as helping people feel they live in the midst of the two embraces of God's love: the gracious love of the Father who made us his children at baptism, and the merciful love of the Father who continuously calls us back when we have turned away from him. We are God's children, but like the prodigal son we have often shunned his love and gone astray. The preacher's main mission is to constantly call us to encounter Christ anew, to rejoice in our Christian identity as God's children, to consider how we have turned away from the Father's love and the ways in which the Father may be calling us back to his loving embrace, welcoming us back home (EG 144).

> *The effort one puts into preaching is an expression of love for God and for God's people.*

This Christian identity, as the baptismal embrace which the Father gave us when we were little ones, makes us desire, as prodigal children … yet another embrace, that of the merciful Father who awaits us in glory. Helping our people to feel that they live in the midst of these two embraces is the difficult but beautiful task of one who preaches the Gospel. (EG 144)

The Painful Homily

The homily should set hearts on fire. It is meant to be a happy experience, an encounter with God's Word, and a continuous source of renewal and growth for our lives (EG 136). Some preachers do this well, but Pope Francis humorously notes that the homily is not always such a joyful experience.

> The homily is the touchstone for judging a pastor's closeness and ability to communicate with his people. We know that the faithful attach great importance to it, and that both they and their ordained minsters suffer because of homilies: the laity from having to listen to them and the clergy from having to preach them! (EG 135)

When homilies are not connecting with the people, preachers might be tempted to blame the parishioners saying, they don't listen, they don't care, or they are distracted. But Pope Francis challenges preachers to consider what they can do differently, taking the time, especially if they have never done so, to discover effective ways to shape and offer the message. And yet the effort one puts into preaching — the tapping into every creative effort, every talent — is an expression of love for God and for God's people. Essentially, it is an act of love to offer the best possible homily rather than an inferior product (156).

But Pope Francis doesn't just challenge preachers to deliver better homilies, he offers practical tips on how to do this.

1. Keep It Brief

Situated within the liturgy, the homily should be concise and should definitely not be a lecture. Even if the preacher is engaging and can hold people's attention for an hour, a long homily can detract from the liturgy with the result that the preacher's words become the center of attention (EG 138). Francis turns to

Scripture to find good advice on how to develop a homily that will best touch the hearts of the people: "Speak concisely, say much in few words" (*Sir* 32:8).

2. Remember, It's Not a Form of Entertainment

As a part of the Mass, the homily is not just a presentation on the faith. The words of the homily actually become "part of the offering made to the Father and a mediation of the grace which Christ pours out during the celebration." The preaching, therefore, should lead people to the profound communion they will have with Jesus in the Eucharist. Stories, images, personal testimony, and even a prudent touch of humor might be employed to draw people into the Word of God or illustrate points. The preacher, however, should never feel he needs to entertain the people; that would be to put the spotlight on himself, not on Christ. Hence, "the words of the preacher must be measured, so that the Lord, more than his minister, will be the center of attention" (EG 138).

3. It Is Heart-to-Heart Communication, Not Just Teaching

If the preacher is to deepen the dialogue between God and His people, he must remember that dialogue entails more than communicating an abstract truth. "A preaching which would be purely moralistic or doctrinaire, or one which turns into a lecture on biblical exegesis, detracts from this heart-to-heart communication" (EG 142). The goal is not simply to download doctrinal points, pass on information, or help people pass a catechism quiz. The aim of a homily, Pope Francis says, is to enkindle within the hearts of the people a desire to be more united with the heart of God. In order to achieve this goal, the preacher needs to know his people — where they are on fire with the love of God and where their dialogue with God has grown cold (EG 137).

4. Proclaim a Synthesis, Not Detached Ideas

Pope Francis challenges the preacher to discover the principal message of the Biblical text that gives the passage its structure and unity. And he should link the main theme to the larger Gospel message of the Catholic faith: God's love for us made manifest in Jesus Christ. If the preacher fails to focus on one central theme, he'll end up with unrelated ideas that will lack organization, fall flat, and fail to inspire (EG 147). Preachers have the opportunity to show how themes from the readings fit into the larger story of salvation. Proclaiming a synthesis thus highlights the unity of the faith and reinforces the basic Gospel message that should always be on the preacher's lips: "Jesus Christ loves you; he gave his life to save you; and now he is living at your side every day to enlighten, strengthen, and free you" (EG 164).

The ability to successfully proclaim a synthesis can make or break a homily. Without a thematic unity, we are left with scattered ideas, disjointed points. The homily becomes disorganized, trying to cover too many things at once, and people are not able to easily follow the line of argument. "Where your synthesis is, there lies your heart. The difference between enlightening people with a synthesis and doing so with detached ideas is like the difference between boredom and heartfelt fervor" (EG 143).

5. Take Time to Prepare: Humility before God's Word

The preacher must have "a humble and awe-filled veneration" of the Bible, one that approaches the Scripture readings with a profound reverence, recognizing he is encountering not any ordinary book, but the inspired Word of God. The humble heart knows that God's Word is always beyond him. He needs God's help to understand it, to know what should be preached and how best to communicate that to the people. This reverence for God's Word should drive him to study it "with the greatest care and a holy fear lest we distort it" (EG 146). But this requires time.

Dedicating quality time to homily preparation must be a priority. Adequate time should be set aside for prayerful study of the Word of God and homily preparation, even if that means allocating less time to other important works. "To interpret a biblical text, we need to be patient, to put aside all other concerns, and to give it our time, interest and undivided attention.

We must leave aside any other pressing concerns and create an environment of serene concentration" (EG 146).

And preachers should not take short-cuts when preparing a homily or any teaching of the faith. Quickly reading the Biblical text, searching for quick and easy results, is not fruitful. Failure to take sufficient time to prayerfully reflect on the Scripture readings and prepare a homily may not simply be a sign of busyness ("I just don't have time!"), it may also indicate a lack of humility before God's Word. If we truly recognized how much we need the help of the Holy Spirit to understand the inspired words of Scripture and guide our homily preparation, we wouldn't try to do it quickly or off the cuff. "Preparation for preaching requires love. We only devote periods of quiet time to the things or the people whom we love, and here we are speaking of the God whom we love, a God who wishes to speak to us" (EG 146).

6. The Preacher Himself Must Be Challenged by God's Word

Preparing a good homily (and again, any teaching of the faith) begins with the preacher's own personal encounter with God in the Scriptures. Some preachers, however, rush into thinking about what they want to teach others without considering how the biblical text applies to their own lives.

But Pope Francis reminds the preacher to allow the Word of God to challenge him deeply, to penetrate and shape his own life first. In this way, preaching will be, in the words of St. Thomas Aquinas, "communicating to others what one has contemplated" (EG 150).[44]

Pope Francis recommends the traditional, prayerful reading of Scripture known as *lectio divina*. In addition to study of the central message of a Biblical text, this recollected reading of the Bible helps us discern how that message applies to our own lives. We allow God's word to speak to us personally, to enlighten, challenge, and renew us. He gives some examples of the kinds of questions one should talk to God about while reflecting on the Biblical text in this way:

Lord, what does this text say *to me*? What is it about my life that you want to change by this text? What troubles me about this text? Why am I not interested in this? Or perhaps: What do I find pleasant in this text? What is it about this word that moves me? What attracts me? Why does it attract me? (EG 153)

When the preacher contemplates the sacred text in this way, it will have a more profound effect on his preaching. "The Sunday readings will resonate in all their brilliance in the hearts of the faithful if they have first done so in the heart of their pastor" (EG 149). The people listening, therefore, will know that they are hearing from clergy who speak of a God they intimately know.

Pope Francis warns preachers not to avoid this personal encounter with God's Word: "Yet if he does not take time to hear God's word with an open heart, if he does not allow it to touch his life, to challenge him, to impel him, and if he does not devote time to pray with that word, then he will indeed be a false prophet, a fraud, a shallow imposter" (EG 151).

7. Contemplate Your Community

Contemplating Scripture is foundational, but the preacher also must take time to "contemplate his people" (EG 123). Does he really know his people — their hopes and fears, their joys and disappointments in life? Does he really know what they are going through, what weighs on their hearts, their daily struggles? Does he know where they are in their relationship with God — how they have matured in their faith and what keeps them from taking the next step in entrusting their lives more to Christ?

Preaching in the abstract alone is not very effective. Giving a very clear explanation of certain doctrinal or moral points while failing to connect those points to people's daily lives will not make a good homily. Pope Francis encourages preachers to think of human experiences such as reunions, disappointments, isolation, entering into the sufferings of others, worry about the future. "We need to develop a broad and profound sensitivity to what really affects other people's lives" (EG 155).

The more preachers go out and have contact with their people, the more they will understand the way they live, the way they pray, the way they look at the world, the way they understand God, the way they approach work, friendship, marriage, family life, leisure, entertainment. All this helps the preacher connect the biblical text to his people's real life situations (EG 154).

Questions for Reflection

1. Pope Francis says that when preparing to teach the Scriptures, we need to give it our full attention, set aside every concern that distracts us, and carve out the time and the peaceful environment that will allow us to focus (EG 146). Why is this so important for teaching the Scriptures? How well do you do in humbly giving God this kind of effort when preparing to teach the faith? What can we do to make preparation in God's Word more of a priority?

2. For those in any role of teaching the faith, including parents: Do you allow yourself to be personally challenged by God's Word before you teach it others? In other words, do you take time to encounter God in the Scriptures, prayerfully asking Him, "Lord, what does this text say *to me?*" Or do you turn to the Scriptures and the *Catechism* more for information to pass on to others? What can you do to allow yourself daily to be challenged by God's Word?

3. Pope Francis says we must teach a synthesis, not isolated ideas. What would be an example of teaching detached ideas? What would be an example of teaching a synthesis?

4. Francis says the preacher must "contemplate his people" to understand what people go through — their hopes, questions, struggles, and fears (EG 123). Why is this important for teaching the faith? How much time do you spend contemplating the people in your care and listening to them?

CHAPTER TEN

A PROPHETIC COUNTER-CULTURAL WITNESS

Living in Solidarity with the Poor

Blessed Mother Teresa used to say that the Gospel can be summed up on five fingers. She would point to each finger and recite the five words of Jesus: "You-did-it-to-me." She, of course, was drawing on the famous passage in the Gospel of Matthew, chapter twenty-five, about how those who provide for the hungry, welcome the stranger, clothe the naked, and visit the sick perform these charitable acts ultimately for Christ. When we give to the poor, it is as if we are giving to God, who is especially present in the poor. "Truly, I say to you, as you did it to one of the least of these my brethren, you did it to me" (Mt 25:40).

Pope Francis worries that the simplicity of this call to fraternal charity is something that Christians take for granted. Most of us are able to recite Christ's teaching to "love your neighbor as yourself," but not all of us allow this teaching to shape our lives. "How dangerous and harmful this is, for it makes us lose our amazement, our excitement, and our zeal for living the Gospel of fraternity and justice!" (EG 179). The pope beautifully describes how "our brothers and sisters are the prolongation of the incarnation for each of us" (EG 179). But do we try to encounter Jesus in our neighbor, especially in those who need our help the most?

In this chapter, we will see how care for those in need through the works of mercy is not only a key criterion for Christian authenticity. It's also a crucial counter-cultural witness in the New Evangelization.

A New Mindset

Love of neighbor, Pope Francis says, is "the clearest sign for discerning spiritual growth in response to God's completely free gift" (EG 179). Throughout *The Joy of the Gospel,* he cites dozens of Scriptural passages that call us to solidarity with those in need. God loves the poor so much he became one of them. He was laid in a manger like a poor child, and born into a poor family who at the Presentation could not even afford the lamb normally required for the sacrifice (Lk 2:24). Jesus himself said he came to preach good news to the poor (Lk 4:18), associated with the poor throughout his public ministry, died as a poor man on Calvary, and continues to identify himself with the poor today, saying, "As you did it to one of these, the least of my brethren, you did it to me" (Mt 25:40).

> *We are called to "a new mindset which thinks in terms of community."*
> — *Pope Francis*

The message is clear: Our relationship with the poor and suffering directly affects our relationship with God: "If anyone has the world's goods and sees his brother in need, yet closes his heart against him, how does God's love abide in him?" (1 Jn 3:17).

But this is not a call merely to volunteer one evening at a soup kitchen or give a little more money to the poor. Pope Francis says Scripture invites us to something more than just occasional scattered gestures of service (EG 188), or "a kind of 'charity á la carte,' or a series of acts aimed solely at easing our conscience" (EG 180). We are called to "a *new mindset* which thinks in terms of community and the priority of the life of all," not just our own self-interest (EG 188, emphasis added).

The "Throw Away" Culture

When we take on this communal perspective, it challenges us to evaluate seriously the way we relate to money and possessions. Today we are often "reduced to one ... [need] alone: consumption" (EG 55) — to buy more, have more, and store up more, much more than we really need. We think this will make us happy, but it leaves us empty and hankering to move on to the next stimulating purchase, while many others struggle to survive day-to-day. Pope Francis calls us to honestly consider

> "Not to share one's wealth with the poor is to steal from them."
> — St. John Chrysostom

how deeply this consumerist culture has affected us. How much are we driven to find fulfillment in earning more, purchasing more, saving more? Do we fall into wastefulness? How does our behavior contribute to the "throw away" culture? How much have we allowed money to have dominion over us?

When we adopt this Christian communal mindset, however, we no longer see our wealth as our own — something to protect, cling to, and use just for our own purposes. We begin to see it as a gift that God entrusts to us to serve a common good. Indeed, the Scriptures teach that we are stewards called to faithfully manage the Lord's gifts so that they can be put to good service for the kingdom of God. In this light, almsgiving can be seen as not so much about giving up "my" money to help other people, but about being a good steward of the Lord's blessings, using them as he desires. Pope Francis quotes Pope Paul VI who said "the more fortunate should renounce some of their rights so as to place their goods more generously at the service of others."[45]

However, when we view our wealth merely as our own to use however selfishly we please, we don't simply withhold mercy, we commit an injustice. Francis quotes St. John Chrysostom on this point: "Not to share one's wealth with the poor is to steal from them and to take away their livelihood. It is not our goods which we hold, but theirs" (EG 57).

The Scriptures even teach that showing mercy to those in need helps atone for sin (cf. Dan 4:27; 1 Pet 4:8), and that almsgiving "will purge away every sin" (Tob. 12:9), further motivation to serve Jesus in the poor. Pope Francis quotes St. Augustine's reflection on the statement in the Book of Sirach: "Water extinguishes a blazing fire: so almsgiving atones for sin" (Sir 3:30):

> If we were in peril from fire, we would certainly run to water in order to extinguish the fire ... in the same way, if a spark of sin flares up from our straw, and we are troubled on that account, whenever we have an opportunity to perform a work of mercy, we should rejoice, as if a fountain opened before so that the fire might be extinguished.[46]

A Prophetic Counter-Cultural Resistance

This was all part of the communal mindset of the early Christians, and one that formed "a prophetic, counter-cultural resistance to the self-centered hedonism of paganism" (EG 193). So important was care for the poor that the apostles made it a key standard by which to measure Christian identity. When St. Paul wanted to make sure he was being faithful to the Gospel, for example, he presented to the apostles in Jerusalem the message he was preaching to the gentiles. They extended to him "the right hand of fellowship," but the chief criterion the apostles gave him for his mission to the gentiles was to "remember the poor" (cf. Gal. 2:10).

This care for the poor was a crucial mark of authentic faith, and one that would make Paul's Christian communities throughout Asia Minor and Greece very different from the self-centered, hedonistic culture around them. Radiant with fraternal charity, especially toward society's most vulnerable, the early Christian communities bore witness to the love of Christ. But their works of mercy were not just a nice thing to do. They were, as Pope Francis said, prophetic and counter-cultural, pointing to the fullness of life in community to which we are all called.

As a new pagan culture emerges in our own day, Pope Francis summons us to give the same kind of Christian witness, caring for the weak and vulnerable — the homeless, the addicted, refugees, indigenous peoples, immigrants, the unborn, the elderly (EG 210, 213). He holds up the example of Paul's Christian communities, which did "not succumb to the self-centered lifestyle of the pagans" as a crucial model for us to follow today. "We may not always be able to reflect adequately the beauty of the Gospel, but there is one sign which we should never lack: the option for those who are least, those whom society discards" (EG 195).

Not for Everyone?

But is it realistic to expect all Christians to care for the poor? Does this apply to everyone? As a theology professor, I, for example, might say that I am focused on training people for the New Evangelization. I might encourage *them* to serve the poor, and then I might throw a few extra bills in the second collection basket at church. But is directly caring for the poor something I need to do myself? Moreover, as a husband and father of seven children, I also have a full plate of responsibilities at home. Much of family life, especially when the kids are younger, is all about the works of mercy: I constantly feed the hungry, clothe the naked, fill up sippy cups for the thirsty, visit the sick, and come to those in the childhood prison called "time out"! How would I have time to go downtown and care for the poor?

Pope Francis' teaching and his personal witness of serving the poor is quite challenging. He comes right out and says, "No one must say that they cannot be close to the poor because their own lifestyle demands more attention to other areas" (EG 201). He laments that this excuse is often given by academics, business people, and other professionals, and even among those working in the Church. He concludes that no one is exempt from caring for the poor (EG 201). Indeed, a Christian community that lacks this urgent desire to show mercy tends to turn in on itself. "Any Church community, if it thinks it can comfortably go its own way without creative concern and effective cooperation in help-ing the poor to live with dignity and reaching out to everyone, will also risk breaking down.... It will easily drift into spiritual worldliness camouflaged by religious practices, unproductive meetings, and empty talk" (EG 207).

Serving the poor will take a variety of forms for different people, but Pope Francis challenges every one of us to do some-thing to draw closer to the poor and vulnerable among us. And, as we saw in chapter six, he wants us to do more than give money — he wants us to personally *encounter* those in need. Such an *encuentro* not only makes a difference for the people we serve, but a transformation also begins to occur in our own heart. In the words of Pope Benedict XVI, we become "conquered by love." Through charitable works, Christians are to become "persons moved by Christ's love, persons whose hearts Christ has con-quered with his love, awakening within them a love of neighbor" (*Deus Caritas Est*, 33).

Questions for Reflection

1. How much has the consumerist culture affected you? Hon-estly consider how much you are driven to earn more mon-ey, save more, or purchase more than you really need? To what extent do you participate in the "throw away culture"?

2. In what ways do you think serving the poor is "a prophetic, counter-cultural resistance" to the self-centered hedonism of our world today? How well are you giving this prophetic witness of service to the poor?

3. St. John Chrysostom said that when we don't share our wealth with the poor we steal from them: "It is not our goods which we hold, but theirs." Do you tend to view your wealth as merely your own or as a gift from God en-trusted to you for the sake of others as well? How do you demonstrate that in everyday living?

THE DEEP BREATH OF PRAYER

Spirit-Filled Evangelizers for the New Evangelization

There is much discussion about the New Evangelization being new in ardor, new in methods, and new in expressions.

These characteristics, first articulated by Pope St. John Paul II,[47] may encourage people to develop new programs, start new initiatives, or use new technologies to proclaim the Gospel. But it would be a mistake to view the New Evangelization as being primarily about our own creativity, energy, and effort, as if *we* were the ones all on our own stirring up a new ardor and coming up with new methods and expressions to proclaim the faith. Pope Francis emphasizes that while the New Evangelization will demand much from us, it is not an "individual heroic effort." It is ultimately the Lord's work. "The real newness is the newness which God himself mysteriously brings about and inspires, provokes, guides and accompanies in a thousand ways" (EG 12).

The source of the New Evangelization, therefore, is not our own human ingenuity, planning, scheming, and hard work, but our personal encounter with Jesus Christ and our own ongoing conversion. From this daily encounter with the Lord, the Holy Spirit subtly inspires, guides, and encourages the faithful to give themselves more to others, to share their own joy in the Gospel, and to do so in ways that meet the needs of our time. "Whenever we make the effort to return to the source and to recover the original freshness of the Gospel, new avenues arise, new paths of creativity open up, with different forms of expression, more eloquent signs and words with new meaning from today's world. Every form of authentic evangelization is always 'new'" (EG 11). In this way, the work of the New Evangelization is ultimately not our own. It is Christ working through us.

The Divine Initiative

The Church is a pilgrim people — a people who were created by God and who are on a journey toward God. God draws us to himself and invites us to be instruments of evangelization drawing others toward Him as well. God takes the initiative to seek us out. He *longs* for all humanity to be united with him. We are invited to participate in that divine longing, to share in God's love for our brothers and sisters in the human family. Pope Francis quotes an amazing statement from his predecessor Pope Benedict XVI on this point: "It is important always to know that the first word, the true initiative, the true activity comes from God, and only by inserting ourselves into the divine initiative, only by begging for this divine initiative, shall we too be able to become — with him and in him — evangelizers."[48]

> *"Only by begging for this divine initiative, shall we too be able to become — with him and in him — evangelizers."*
> — *Pope Benedict XVI*

This teaching makes clear that we must *beg* for this divine initiative, lest we build our own projects and not the Lord's. When we undertake an apostolic work, some of us might just rush in to begin the task without seeking God's guidance. Some of us might take time to say a short prayer at the start, but then we run off to the races to get the work done without an ongoing dialogue with the Lord underlying all we do.

Pope Francis challenges us to ask how much time we truly take to encounter God in prayer and how much we allow God's initiative to permeate all that we do. Do we create that interior space in our daily lives to be attentive to the Holy Spirit's promptings? Do we actually "beg" God for his inspiration? Do we beg him to keep us from being trapped in our own limited human perspectives, fears, or self-interests? Do we beg him to keep us from going astray in our work?

Pope Francis says evangelization must be guided by the Holy Spirit. And if we are going to be evangelizers who are filled with the Spirit, prayer must be at the heart of all we do or our efforts will yield little fruit. We are called to give people far more than dynamic presentations, eloquent explanations, or well-organized events. "Jesus wants evangelizers who proclaim the good news not only with words, but above all by a life transfigured by God's presence" (EG 259).

Here are some of the practical ways Pope Francis calls us to be Spirit-filled evangelizers:

1. The Deep Breath of Prayer

Pope Francis says spirit-filled evangelizers must cultivate "interior space" amid their work. He has in mind something more than saying a few occasional prayers or devotions such as the rosary, novenas, and the Divine Mercy chaplet. He even has in mind something in addition to the liturgical life of the Church, morning and evening prayer, or the Mass.

Vocal prayers, devotions, and above all the liturgy certainly should be part of the Christian's spiritual life. But Pope Francis calls us to make sure we also set aside time for intimate, daily conversation with the Lord — a personal dialogue with Him and a daily encounter with his saving love. He calls us to take in "the deep breath of prayer" that comes from meditation on God's word, prayerfully reflecting on it, talking to God about it, and asking the Lord how it applies to our life. From this deep breath of prayer flow joyful praise, thanksgiving, and intercession for others.

For our daily prayer, we might reflect on passages from the Bible or the Scripture readings from Mass. Or we might feed our meditation with resources that provide reflections on the Christian life such as *My Daily Bread, Magnificat,* or the spiritual classic *The Imitation of Christ.* Our prayer at times might also entail just quietly resting in God's presence with open hearts, allowing him to gaze lovingly upon us: "How good it is to stand before a crucifix, or on our knees before the Blessed Sacrament, and simply be in his presence!" (EG 264). Pope Francis particularly recommends Eucharistic adoration as a powerful moment of encounter with Our Lord in the Blessed Sacrament. Whatever the setting might be, it's crucial that we make time for this intimate conversation with the Lord each day. "Without prolonged moments of adoration, of prayerful encounter with the word, of sincere conversation with the Lord, our work easily becomes meaningless; we lose energy as a result of weariness and difficulties, and our fervor dies out" (EG 262).

> *"Yet there is no greater freedom than that of allowing oneself to be guided by the Holy Spirit, renouncing the attempt to plan and control everything to the last detail."*
> — Pope Francis

2. Plunged into the Deep

A second way to be Spirit-filled evangelizers is to cultivate a deep trust in the work and presence of the Holy Spirit (EG 280). Pope Francis invites us to invoke the Holy Spirit constantly, asking the Spirit to guide our decisions, shape our lives, and help us in the trials we face. Giving up control and allowing ourselves to be led by the Spirit, however, can be frightening and disorienting, but it is also very freeing, since the Holy Spirit knows better than we what is needed in every situation:

> It is like being plunged into the deep and not knowing what we will find. I myself have frequently experienced this. Yet there is no greater freedom than that of allowing

oneself to be guided by the Holy Spirit, renouncing the attempt to plan and control everything to the last detail, and instead letting him enlighten, guide and direct us, leading us wherever he wills. (EG 280)

When we give up our own plans, implore the Spirit to guide us, and follow the Spirit's promptings, our apostolic work is more fruitful. Indeed, our work in evangelization is not our own. It is Christ's Spirit working through us.

3. Resurrection Hope

Spirit-filled evangelizers are not gloomy or discouraged. They are convinced that "God is able to act in every situation," no matter what obstacles, setbacks, or trials they may face. Even in the midst of great indifference and evil, the Christian has confidence that God is still present in the world, inspiring new lights to shine in the darkness. "Goodness always reemerges," and human beings rise again from situations that seemed hopeless. History bears witness over and over again to Christ's resurrection triumphing in the end over evil (EG 279, 276).

Pope Francis says all who evangelize are instruments of the power of the resurrection, and we should never lack confidence in the risen Christ, who marches through history looking for disciples who will march with him in extending his Kingdom. "Christ's resurrection everywhere calls forth seeds of that new world; even if they are cut back, they grow again, for the resurrection is already secretly woven into the fabric of this history, for Jesus did not rise in vain" (EG 278).

We may not always notice the fruit of our labors, but as spirit-filled evangelizers, we should possesses an interior certainty that if we have lovingly entrusted ourselves to God we will bear good fruit even if we cannot see it. "No single act of love for God will be lost; no generous effort is meaningless; no painful endurance is wasted" (EG 279). The fruitfulness of our apostolic work cannot be easily measured. The fruits may be the mustard seed that later becomes the large tree. Our crosses and sacrifices may help people of a later time or in a different part of the world. "Let us keep marching forward; let us give him everything, allowing him to make our efforts bear fruit in his good time" (EG 279).

4. Making Our Prayer "Full of People"

Pope Francis says that if we were to look inside St. Paul's heart while he was praying, we would see that it was "full of people." Indeed, Paul himself told his followers, "I thank my God every time I remember you, constantly praying with joy in every one of my prayers for all of you" (Phil 1:3–4, NAB)."

Paul's letters are packed with two kinds of prayers for his people: thanksgiving and intercession.

Paul began his letters *thanking God for his people*: "I thank my God through Jesus Christ for all of you" (Rom 1:8). "I give thanks to God always for you" (1 Cor 1:4). "I thank my God in all my remembrance of you" (Phil 1:3). Such prayers of gratitude flow from attentiveness to others and help us recognize how God is working in people's lives. When we pray in thanksgiving for others in this way, we rise out of our self-centeredness and are more inclined to share our lives with them (EG 282).

Intercessory prayer for people and their needs is also a hallmark of Paul's writings. Pope Francis notes how St. Paul and all the saints were powerful intercessors who trusted that their prayers really made a difference. The pope describes these intercessory prayers as "'leaven' in the heart of the Trinity" that penetrate the Father's heart and can shed divine light on difficult situations and bring about change. "We can say that God's heart is touched by our intercession, yet in reality he is always there first. What our intercession achieves is that his power, his love and his faithfulness are shown ever more clearly in the mindset of the people" (EG 283).

5. Desire to Be "In the Heart of People"

The Spirit inspires evangelizers with an ardent desire to be with people, to be close to their lives (EG 268). We may notice a desire to live more fully with the people around us, to listen to their concerns, to rejoice in what brings them joy, to weep with those who weep. This is the Spirit drawing us out of ourselves and more into the hearts of others (EG 273).

This sharing in other people's lives is not something extra we do as Christians or a task to accomplish only within our formal apostolic work. It's at the very heart of our mission as disciples: "*I am a mission* on this earth; that is the reason why I am here in this world. We have to regard ourselves as sealed, even branded, by this mission of bringing light, blessing, enlivening, raising up, healing, and freeing" (EG 273).

Our life as missionary disciples is not something that we can take off like a badge when we leave the parish property. We bring our faith out into the world, into everything we do, giving witness to Christ. When we do this, the world becomes full of teachers, politicians, nurses, and others with "soul," the pope says, who bring Christ's light into the workplace and public sphere. And through their life of committed concern for others, they contribute to building up a civilization of love (EG 273).

6. Sharing the One We Love with Others

Spirit-filled evangelizers are convinced, not just intellectually, but from their own personal experience, that Jesus Christ makes all the difference in their lives. And this is the reason we desire to proclaim the Gospel: to share our joy in Him.

To persevere in a life-long mission of evangelization, we must be convinced "that it is not the same thing to have known Jesus as not to have known him, not the same thing to walk with him as to walk blindly,... not the same thing to try to build the world with his Gospel as to try to do so by our own lights. We know well that with Jesus life becomes richer and that with him it is easier to find meaning in everything. This is why we evangelize" (EG 266).

Such a conviction that Christ makes all the difference in life only comes from our own personal discipleship with the Lord day-to-day — to encounter him humbly in our weakness, to receive his mercy and forgiveness over and over again, and to experience his saving help, liberating us from our sins, opening doors that were closed, and guiding us in our apostolic work. A true missionary never stops being a disciple. Jesus is with him and he knows it — walking with him, speaking to him, always with him, as close as his breath (EG 266). And from this conviction, born of his own personal, ongoing experience of God's love, he cannot help but make his Beloved known to others.

If we find, however, that we do not have a fervent desire to evangelize — to make the One we love known to others — it may be a sign that our soul has become lukewarm, and we won't be an effective witness to Jesus Christ: We won't convince anyone if we're not convinced ourselves — in love and full of enthusiasm and certainty (EG 266).

This is a dangerous spiritual position in which to find ourselves. Pope Francis says if we fall into this spiritual and apostolic complacency, we need to beg God for help: "We need to pray insistently that he will once more touch our hearts. We need to implore his grace daily, asking him to open our cold hearts and shake up our lukewarm and superficial existence" (EG 264). We need to encounter Christ anew, like Matthew the tax collector, hearing Our Lord call us to let go of whatever money bags remain in our clutch and follow him in discipleship.

7. Like Mary — Contemplation and Service

Pope Francis concludes *The Joy of the Gospel* reflecting on how Mary models for us the New Evangelization. Mary gave her "yes" to the Lord in her *fiat* at the Annunciation, and she continuously renewed her *fiat* throughout her life, through trials, uncertainties, and ultimately the cross. She kept and pondered all things in her heart (Lk 2:19). She proved to be a faithful disciple, walking with the Lord step-by-step from Nazareth all the way to the cross. Flowing from this ongoing encounter with the God "who has done great things" for her (Lk 1:49), Mary went out and shared the love of the Lord that she experienced with others. She went out, took initiative, and showed concern for those in need (Lk 1:39; Jn 2:3). She shared her joy with others (Lk 1:44) and proclaimed God's greatness.

Indeed, Mary is the "star of the New Evangelization." Pope Francis prays that she will "help us to bear radiant witness to communion, service, ardent and generous faith, justice and love of the poor, that the joy of the Gospel may reach to the ends of the earth, illuminating even the fringes of our world" (EG 288).

Questions for Reflection

1. Pope Francis says, "There is no greater freedom than that of allowing oneself to be guided by the Holy Spirit, renouncing the attempt to plan and control everything to the last detail." While planning and organizing certainly is important, how might the pope's statement challenge you to be more open to allowing the Spirit to guide and direct your apostolic efforts?

2. Why is daily prayer — a daily personal encounter with the Lord — crucial for anyone working in the New Evangelization? What happens to our apostolic work when we fail to take time for the "deep breath of prayer" each day?

3. Pope Francis says we should make our prayer "full of people" — thanking God for the people in our care and interceding for them constantly. Take time now to consider those people in your care: Can you thank God for them? For what, in particular? What petitions can you bring to God for them? Then make a resolution to pray in thanksgiving and intercession for these people each day.

Appendix

An Outline of Pope Francis' *The Joy of the Gospel*

In this appendix, we will step back and consider the "big picture" of *The Joy of the Gospel* — its overarching themes and how those themes are developed throughout the document.

The Problem
"Ecclesial Introversion"

One interpretive key to *The Joy of the Gospel* is Pope Francis' concern that the Church not close in on itself. He urgently calls us to move from a pastoral ministry of "mere conservation" to a pastoral approach that on every level is decidedly missionary (EG 15), one that does not let us passively wait in our church buildings, but launches us out into the peripheries to reach those who are in need of the Gospel (EG 20). He quotes Pope St. John Paul II, who warned that the Church must not fall into "ecclesial introversion" (EG 27).[49] The Church must not focus on itself but on Christ and on bringing His saving love to the world.

The Solution
Encounter with Christ and with God's People

To avoid the danger of "ecclesial introversion," Pope Francis invites us to a double encounter: an encounter with Christ and an encounter with the people we serve. Through a renewed personal encounter with Jesus Christ, we are drawn out of ourselves — our fears, weaknesses, self-centeredness, and sins — and brought to the fullness of life found in living for God and others. And through a personal encounter with our neighbor — whether it be the poor, those who do not know friendship with Christ, or the people God has placed in our daily lives — we are drawn out of our self-centered lifestyles and closer to the people around us, as we radiate the love of Christ that we ourselves have encountered.

———————

This central message of *The Joy of the Gospel* is to be carried out on three levels: the individual, the Church, and the world. These three levels correspond to the first three major sections of the document.

The Joy of the Gospel — Introduction
Individual Renewal

In the introduction to his apostolic exhortation, Pope Francis summons each individual Christian to a renewed personal encounter with Christ (EG 2). He asks us to humbly come before Jesus each day, confessing our sins and weaknesses, admitting the thousand ways we shun his love, asking his forgiveness, and begging for his saving help. This on-going conversion is at the heart of a disciple who seeks to imitate Christ and surrender ever more of his life to him.

And this discipleship leads to mission: The true disciple knows at the core of his being how much of a difference friendship with Christ makes. He has experienced Christ's saving love, liberating him from his self-absorption and sin. He has experienced the joy of the Gospel and is driven to share this joy. "For if we have received the love which restores meaning to our lives, how can we fail to share that love with others?" (EG 8).

The Joy of the Gospel — Chapter 1
Renewal of the Church

Pope Francis also calls for the missionary "conversion" of the Church as a whole, so that all the Church's structures, customs, schedules, and ways of doing things are directed to going out to the peripheries and evangelizing. Those doing apostolic work must step out of their comfort zones and go out to all those who need the light of the Gospel, rather than sitting back and waiting for people to come to them (EG 19–33).

This mission to go out into the world has three main consequences. First, it shapes the way we communicate the faith, focusing on the heart of the Gospel message (EG 34–39). Second, it shapes our approach as we work in the midst of various human limitations that invite us to greater patience, generosity, and prudence (EG 40–45). Finally, it challenges us in the Church to move from a pastoral strategy that aims merely at maintaining things as they currently are to an approach that urgently seeks to share friendship with Christ with those who don't know Him (EG 46–49).

The Joy of the Gospel — Chapter 2
Renewal of the World

If we renew our encounter with Christ (Introduction) and are sent on mission to go out and share Christ's saving love with the world (Chapter One), it will be important to understand the cultural landscape in which we carry out our mission. That comes in the second chapter, titled "Amid the Crisis of Communal Commitment." Here, Pope Francis laments the pervasive individualism in the modern world that encourages people to focus on self and not on God and others. Caught up in their own pursuit of wealth, pleasure, entertainment, and success, many people shun their responsibilities toward others.

In the first half of this chapter (EG 50–75), he notes how this individualism causes an array of social problems, including the exclusion of the poor from society, the breakdown in marriage and the family, and moral relativism. But in the second half (EG 76–109), the pope says many believers in the Church also fall prey to the self-centered spirit of our age. Even some of those formally working in the Church can be more concerned about protecting their free time, safeguarding their positions of influence, pursuing comfort and wealth, and seeking recognition and applause than they are about throwing their lives entirely into the Church's mission. This not only prevents them from experiencing the fullness of life found in Christ's self-giving love. It also hinders their ability to participate in the Church's mission. It leads them to be driven more by self-interest ("What's in it for me?") than by a desire to evangelize.

And so we see these three major themes running throughout *The Joy of the Gospel* in its first three sections:

- individual personal renewal,
- the missionary transformation of the Church as a whole,
- and the crisis of communal commitment in our modern world.

Later chapters pick up these motifs and develop them further.

The Joy of the Gospel — Chapter 3
Proclamation (Related to the Church's Missionary Transformation)

The third chapter of the pope's exhortation is called "The Proclamation of the Gospel." It addresses further the main theme of chapter one, the missionary conversion of the Church. Here, Pope Francis explores the foundational call for each believer to participate in the Church's work of evangelization as "missionary disciples" (EG 110–134) and discusses how the Gospel message is presented in the modern world (EG 169–173), how one prepares for that proclamation (see EG 135–159), and how proclamation also demands ongoing formation and personal accompaniment throughout the process of Christian maturity (160–175).

The Joy of the Gospel — Chapter 4
Evangelization's Social Dimension
(Related to the Crisis of Communal Commitment)

The fourth chapter of the apostolic exhortation is on "The Social Dimension of Evangelization." It underscores how love of neighbor and life in community are at the very heart of the Gospel and thus relate to the main problem from chapter two, the crisis of communal commitment (EG 176–185). This section shows further how our solidarity with the poor (EG 186–216) and our work toward peace and the common good (217–258), while always essential, have a special importance amid the "self-centered hedonism" that characterizes our age (EG 193).

The Joy of the Gospel — Chapter 5
Spirit-Filled Evangelizers
(Related to Personal Renewal)

Finally, the fifth chapter of Francis' apostolic exhortation harkens back to the Introduction and the pope's invitation to renew our encounter with Christ. Here at the end, Pope Francis summons each of the faithful to be Spirit-filled evangelizers who encounter Christ's love, who take in the deep breath of prayer, and who are so convinced that life with Christ makes all the difference that they seek to share the Gospel with others (EG 259–267). They want to give their lives entirely to mission, living not for their own purposes, but for the Lord's (268–287).

Notes

1 Anthony Spadaro, "A Big Heart Open to God: The Exclusive Interview with Pope Francis," *America* magazine, September 30, 2013.

2 Ibid.

3 Pope St. John Paul II, Homily at the Shrine of the Holy Cross in Mogila, Poland, June 9, 1979. I am grateful for this insight from my colleague at the Augustine Institute, Professor Doug Bushman. See also Rino Fisichella, *The New Evangelization: Responding to the Challenge of Indifference* (Victoria, Australia: Freedom Publishing, 2012), 18–19.

4 George Weigel, *The End and the Beginning* (New York: Doubleday, 2010), 59.

5 Ibid., 55.

6 Pope St. John Paul II Homily at the Shrine of the Holy Cross in Mogila, Poland, June 9, 1979. www.vatican.va.

7 Ibid.

8 Pope St. John Paul II, Encyclical Letter *Redemptoris Missio*, 33.

9 Cf. Pope St. John Paul II, Apostolic Exhortation *Catechesi Tradendae* (October 16, 1979), 20; Congregation for the Clergy, *General Directory for Catechesis* (August 11, 1997), 53–54.

10 USCCB website.

11 Pope Benedict XVI, "Homily of First Vespers on the Solemnity of the Holy Apostles Peter and Paul," June 28, 2010. www.vatican.va.

12 Pope St. John Paul II, "The Task of the Latin American Bishop," *Origins* 12 (March 24, 1983): 659–62.

13 Synod of Bishops XIII Ordinary General Assembly, *The New Evangelization for the Transmission of Christian Faith, Lineamenta*, 10.

14 *Pope Francis: Our Brother, Our Friend*, ed. Alejandro Bermúdez (San Francisco: Ignatius Press, 2013) 87.

15 Ibid., 71.

16 *Pope Francis: His Life in His Own Words*, eds. Francesca Ambrogetti & Sergio Rubin (New York: Putnam, 2013), 82–83.

17 Ibid., 80–81.

18 Catherine of Siena, Letter to Raymond of Capua (Letter 226) in Mary O'Driscoll, O.P., *Catherine of Siena: Passion for the Truth, Compassion for Humanity* (Hyde Park, NY: New City Press, 1993), p. 36.

19 Nicole Winfield, "Pope ramps up charity office to be near poor, sick" *USA Today* (November 28, 2013). Accessed February 25, 2014. www .usatoday.com/story/news/world/2013/11/28/pope-francis-charity-office/3776499/.

20 Pope Benedict XVI, Address at conclusion of the meeting of the Holy Father with the bishops of Switzerland (November 9, 2006). www .vatican.va.

21 Pope Francis, Address to participants in the meeting organized by the International Federation of Catholic Medical Associations (September 20, 2013). www.vatican.va.

22 This is a point my colleague Sean Innerst has often emphasized. See his doctoral dissertation: Sean Innerst, *The Ancient Narratio as an Ecclesial Participation in the Divine Pedagogy: A Study of its Sources and Proposal for its Current Application* (University of South Africa, November 2010), pp. 287–302. See also: Sean Innerst, "Divine Pedagogy and Covenant Memorial: The Catechetical *Narratio* and the New Evangelization" *Letter & Spirit* 8 (2013): 161–188 (St. Paul Center for Biblical Theology: Steubenville, OH, 2013).

23 Innerst notes more broadly how the canonical arrangement of the New Testament can be seen as reflecting the divine pedagogy with the narrative Gospels and Acts preceding the more detailed doctrinal explications and moral consequences found in the New Testament epistles. Sean Innerst, "Divine Pedagogy and Covenant Memorial: The Catechetical *Narratio* and the New Evangelization" *Letter & Spirit* 8 (2013): 161–188 (St. Paul Center for Biblical Theology: Steubenville, OH, 2013).

24 See Pope St. John Paul II, *Veritatis Splendor*, 81. "If acts are intrinsically evil, a good intention or particular circumstances can diminish their evil, but they cannot remove it." See also CCC 1755–1756: "There are some concrete acts — such as fornication — that it is always wrong to choose, because choosing them entails a disorder of the will, that is, a moral evil…. There are acts which, in and of themselves, independently of circumstances and intentions, are always gravely illicit by reason of their object; such as blasphemy and perjury, murder and adultery."

25 As the *Catechism of the Catholic Church* teaches, "Although we can judge that an act is in itself a grave offense, we must entrust judgment of persons to the justice and mercy of God" (CCC 1861).

26 Cf. CCC 1853.

27 From Genevieve of St. Teresa's testimony during the process of beatification in *St. Thérèse of Lisieux: By Those Who Knew Her*, ed. Christopher O'Mahony (Dublin: Veritas Publications, 1975), p. 132.

28 From Sr. Agnes of Jesus, O.C.D., testimony during the process of beatification in *St. Thérèse of Lisieux: By Those Who Knew Her*, pp. 50–51.

29 St. Catherine of Siena, *The Dialogue*, no. 100, trans. Suzanne Hoffke, O.P. (New York: Paulist Press, 1980), p. 190.

30 Bernard of Clairvaux, *The Steps of Humility and Pride*, 6 in *Bernard of Clairvaux: A Lover Teaching the Way of Love*, ed. M. Basil Pennington (Hyde Park, NY: New City Press, 1997), p. 63. Emphasis added.

31 See Pope St. John Paul II, *Evangelium Vitae, 8*.

32 Pope Francis gave an informal interview with reporters on the airplane returning from World Youth Day in Brazil on July 28, 2013. His comments were reported in, "Who Is Pope Francis to Judge Not?" *Catholic World Report* (March 20, 2014). www.catholicworldreport .com/Item/3013/who_is_pope_francis_to_judge_not.aspx. Accessed April 2, 2014.

33 Pope Francis, Video message to the faithful of Buenos Aires on the occasion of the Feast of St. Cajetan (August 7, 2013). www.news.va. I am grateful for Jonathan Reyes pointing out this quote to me.

34 Mother Teresa's Nobel Prize Address (1979), www.nobelprize.org.

35 Ibid.

36 See mothertheresasayings.com/sayings.htm. Accessed April 2, 2014.

37 Paul VI, *Gaudete in Domino*, 8. See EG 7.

38 Pope Francis, meeting with members of the Pontifical Council for the Family, October 25, 2013, www.catholicnews.com.

39 Pope Francis, Address on the Solemnity of St. Joseph, March 19, 2014.

40 Video Message to the Faithful of Buenos Aires on the Occasion of the Feast of St. Cajetan (August 7, 2013).

41 Second Vatican Council, *Ad Gentes*, 15. CCC 905.

42 Address for the Opening of the Second Vatican Council (October 11, 1962), 4, 2–4, as cited in EG 84.

43 *Dei Verbum*, 24.

44 St. Thomas Aquinas, *S. Th.* II-II, q. 18, a. 6.

45 Paul VI, Apostolic Letter *Octogesima Adveniens*, 23, EG 190.

46 St. Augustine, *De Catechizandis Rudibus*, I, XIX, 22: PL, 40, 327. EG 193.

47 Pope St. John Paul II described the New Evangelization in this way during a 1983 address to the Latin American Episcopal Conference. Address to the Assembly of CELAM (March 9, 1983), III: *AAS* 75 (1983), 778.

48 Meditation during the First General Congregation of the XIII Ordinary General Assembly of the Synod of Bishops (October 8, 2012): AAS 104 (2012), 897. EG 112.

49 Pope St. John Paul II, Post-Synodal Apostolic Exhortation *Ecclesia in Oceania* (November 22, 2001), 19.

About the Author

Dr. Edward Sri is a theologian, author, and nationally known Catholic speaker who appears regularly on EWTN. He has written several Catholic best-selling books, including *A Biblical Walk through the Mass* (Ascension Press). He currently serves as professor of theology and Vice President of Mission at the Augustine Institute in Denver, Colorado.

Dr. Sri is a founding leader with Curtis Martin of FOCUS (Fellowship of Catholic University Students). He also is the host of a new twenty-part video series on the Catholic faith called *Symbolon: The Catholic Faith Explained* (Augustine Institute/Ignatius Press/Lighthouse Catholic Media).

Dr. Sri leads pilgrimages to Rome and the Holy Land and regularly speaks at Catholic parishes, conferences, diocesan catechetical congresses, and clergy retreats. He holds a doctorate from the Pontifical University of St. Thomas Aquinas in Rome and resides with his wife Elizabeth and their seven children in Littleton, Colorado.

Other books by Edward Sri include *Walking with Mary: A Biblical Journey from Nazareth to the Cross* (Image); *The Bible Compass: A Catholic's Guide to Navigating the Scriptures* (Ascension Press); *Men, Women, and the Mystery of Love: Practical Insights on John Paul II's Love and Responsibility* (Servant).